THE
MURDER
OF
MARY
ASHFORD

THE CRIME THAT CHANGED
ENGLISH LEGAL HISTORY

NAOMI CLIFFORD

The Identity of the Killer Finally Revealed...

PEN & SWORD
HISTORY

First published in Great Britain in 2018 by
PEN AND SWORD HISTORY
an imprint of
Pen and Sword Books Ltd
47 Church Street
Barnsley
South Yorkshire S70 2AS

ISBN 978 1 47386 338 5

Printed and bound in England
by CPI Group (UK) Ltd, Croydon, CR0 4YY

Typeset in Times New Roman by
Aura Technology and Software Services, India

Pen & Sword Books Ltd incorporates the imprints of Pen & Sword
Archaeology, Atlas, Aviation, Battleground, Discovery,
Family History, History, Maritime, Military, Naval, Politics, Railways,
Select, Social History, Transport, True Crime, Claymore Press,
Frontline Books, Leo Cooper, Praetorian Press, Remember When,
Seaforth Publishing and Wharncliffe.

For a complete list of Pen and Sword titles please contact
Pen and Sword Books Limited
47 Church Street, Barnsley, South Yorkshire, S70 2AS, England
E-mail: enquiries@pen-and-sword.co.uk
Website: www.pen-and-sword.co.uk

Contents

Measurements

The protagonists in this story understood the importance of the distances quoted in Abraham Thornton's alibi and set about surveying, measuring and recording them in order to prove that certain things could or could not have happened. Although some readers, particularly those of a certain vintage, will have no trouble with miles, yards, feet and inches, this ready reckoner might be helpful for those not brought up using these terms.

    1 mile = 1.6km
    1 yard = 0.91m
    1 foot = 30cm

I have drawn the line at giving distances in furlongs, which are now totally obsolete, and have converted these into yards or fractions of a mile.

Characters

Ann Ashford	Mary Ashford's older sister
Ann Ashford	Mary Ashford's mother
Mary Ashford	Servant working for her uncle John Coleman at Langley Heath
Thomas Ashford	Mary Ashford's father
William Ashford	Mary Ashford's older brother
Thomas Asprey	Lived at Erdington; witness for the prosecution
John Yeend Bedford	Solicitor, nephew of William Bedford
William Bedford	Retired solicitor and Magistrate; lived at Birches Green
William Bedson	Worker at Penns Mill; co-opted as special constable
John Bird	Manager at Penns Mill
Joseph Bird	Worker at Penns Mill; witness for the prosecution
Luke Booker	Vicar of Dudley
Thomas Broadhurst	Witness for the prosecution
John Capper	Superintendent of Prisons and the Hulk Establishment
Benjamin Carter	Erdington farmer; fiancé to Hannah Cox
Joseph Chitty	Legal writer consulted by Ashford side
Daniel Clarke	Keeper of Tyburn House
Nathaniel Gooding Clarke	Prosecution barrister
Charles Coleman	Mary Ashford's uncle, a farmer in Erdington
John Coleman	Mary Ashford's uncle, a farmer at Langley Heath
William Coleman	Mary Ashford's grandfather
Francis Const	Legal writer consulted by Ashford side

CHARACTERS

John Copley	Prosecution barrister
John Cooke	Friend of Thornton
Joseph Cotterill	Friend of Thornton
Hannah Cox	Mary's friend; daughter of Mrs Butler; lived at Erdington Green
John William Crompton	Joseph Webster's brother-in-law
Thomas Dales	Birmingham assistant constable
Joseph Dawson	Labourer; witness for the prosecution
Lord Ellenborough	Lord Chief Justice of England
George Freer	Birmingham surgeon; performed autopsy on Mary Ashford
Francis Beynon Hacket	Sutton Coldfield coroner
John Hackney	Birmingham sheriff's officer
Omar Hall	Convicted felon
Jane Heaton	Servant to John Holden; witness for the defence
John Heydon	Gamekeeper employed by Mr Rotton; witness for the defence
John Hiscox	London attorney
John Holden	Farmer; witness for the defence
Edward Holroyd	Barrister; son of George Sowley Holroyd
George Sowley Holroyd	Judge at Warwick trial
Richard Horton	Sutton Coldfield surgeon; assisted at autopsy
John Humpage	Lived at Witton; witness for the prosecution
John Grant	Head Turnkey at Warwick Gaol
John Gurney	Prosecution barrister (appeal of murder)
George Jackson	Labourer; lived in Birmingham; witness for the prosecution
Martha Jennens	Birmingham milkwoman; witness for the defence
William Jennens	Birmingham milkman; witness for the defence
Fanny Lavell	Wife of William Lavell; laid out Mary's body
William Lavell	Worker at Penns Mill; witness for the prosecution
Alfred Perkins	Prosecution barrister

William Reader	Defence barrister
Henry Revell Reynolds	Defence barrister
Edward Sadler	Attorney for Abraham Thornton
James Simmons	Worker at Penns Mill; witness for the prosecution
Mary Smith	Neighbour of Fanny Lavell
Henry T. Tatnall	Gaoler at Warwick Gaol
Abraham Thornton senior	Builder and farmer of Shard End near Castle Bromwich
Abraham Thornton junior	Bricklayer
Sarah Thornton	Mother of Abraham Thornton junior
Nicholas Conyngham Tindal	Barrister consulted by Thornton side
William Twamley	Gentleman; lived at Newhall Mill near Sutton Coldfield
Zachariah Twamley	Miller of Castle Bromwich
Joseph Webster	Owner of Penns Mill
James White	Witness for the prosecution
John Woodcock	Zachariah Twamley's miller; witness for the defence
George Yates	Clerk to John Yeend Bedford

Introduction

Early one morning I came downstairs to the kitchen to make a cup of tea and noticed, through the French doors, evidence of a crime. On the garden lawn were the remains of a barbeque meal: paper plates, plastic forks and meat bones half hanging out of a bin liner. Convinced that the party held by our neighbour the previous night had got out of hand and someone had lobbed the rubbish bag over the fence, I gathered it up and lobbed it right back. Later that day I found the remains of a bird at the back of the garden and it occurred to me that a fox had dragged the bin bag from next door into our garden and set about devouring it, until distracted by fresher, juicier prey. The neighbours were innocent. This small incident showed me how easy it is to draw the wrong conclusion. Circumstantial evidence, bias against a suspect (the neighbours' party had kept me awake), pressure for a quick solution or simply the desire for a neat ending can lead to error.

Was this the case in the murder of Mary Ashford? After she was found dead in a pit of water in Erdington in 1817 two men who worked at a nearby wire factory looked at footprints in the next-door field and blood drops on the nearby clover and came up with a theory of what had happened to her. They were convinced that the most obvious suspect, a local bricklayer, had murdered her. Members of the local gentry, one of them a magistrate, coordinated the investigation and were equally sure of their man. None of them had training in forensic investigation, which was, in any case, a barely embryonic discipline. Did they interpret the clues correctly? And if they were right, why was Abraham Thornton, the chief suspect, later acquitted, although not exonerated, at his trial?

PART 1

Chapter 1

Discovery

At about six o'clock on the morning of Tuesday 27 May 1817, the day after Whit Monday, George Jackson, as he did every day, took a shortcut through fields from Bell Lane to Penns Mill Lane, just north of the village of Erdington in Warwickshire. His route took him past two marl pits filled with brackish water and it was here, at the second of them, that he saw at the top of the bank, lined up in a row, a bundle bound up with a handkerchief, a bonnet with yellow ribbons and a pair of white leather shoes.

He went to take a look. The bundle contained women's clothes and half-boots. He picked up the white shoes. They were bloodstained. Everything was a little damp from the dew. No doubt he did what anyone would do: he called out, in case the woman lay somewhere nearby injured and in need of help. Silence.

Knowing there were two cottages a short distance away in Penns Mill Lane, he ran to the first. William Lavell, a forty-year-old wire drawer at Penns Mill, was coming out of the door on his way to work but agreed to go back with him to the pit. On their return to the scene Jackson noticed for the first time a trail of blood zig-zagging from the footpath to the pit and what he later described as a 'large lake of blood' in the grass close to a tree. More blood spots were nearby. The two men agreed that Lavell should stay by the pit while Jackson went to Penns Mill half a mile away to raise the alarm. There he found the wire workers gathered in the yard ready to start the day. A few of them, Joseph Bird, James Simmons, Thomas Hiley, John Ray among them, went back to the pit with him, and someone hurried off to inform Joseph Webster, the master.

At the pit, a couple of the volunteers gingerly clambered down the precipitous bank, carefully navigating the briar and overgrowth, to see whether the woman had fallen in. One of them spotted a break in the thick duckweed about a yard from the edge and shouted out that yes, it looked as if someone had gone in there. Then the men clambered up to the field and talked about the best way to get the body out. It was decided that James

Simmons should fetch from his cottage a heel rake and some long reins. The wide edge and strong, curled prongs of the rake would be good for hooking over the body.

Lavell remarked to Jackson that if there was a woman in the pit she must have been thrown in as she had not left any footprints on the slope. By now it was nearly seven o'clock and Jackson, a poor man who worked on the roads, did not want to risk losing pay, so he left the others to it and went on his way.

William Lavell and Joseph Bird went into the neighbouring field to see if it yielded any clues about what had happened. It was likely the woman would have walked from that direction, as Jackson had done, following the public footpath which cut diagonally across, but Lavell soon saw that that had not been not the case. She seemed not to have been on the footpath at all but to have gone around the edge of the field. The farmer had recently ploughed and harrowed the land, leaving rows of neat ridges. In the turned-over soil, around the top of the field, roughly parallel with the lane, were dozens of fresh footprints. The ground was soft, the result of rain the previous week.

She had not been alone. A man, a heavy one judging by the depth of the impressions of his shoes, had been with her. Bird and Lavell tracked the woman and the man to the corner of the field, where there was a dry pit and, turning left, followed them along the edge to the corner of the next field where the footprints rejoined the path. There they saw a patch in the earth, just off the footpath, where there were many footprints.

Afterwards, they went back to look again at the 'lake of blood' and to talk to the men at the pit, and it was then that Lavell saw something he had missed earlier; a single footmark on the steep bank, four or five inches below the edge. He thought it looked like the impression of a man's left foot, pressed hard into the grass. He called Bird over to take a look and told the other men to stay away so as not to ruin the evidence.

William Twamley, a gentleman who lived at Newhall Mill near Sutton Coldfield, was riding along Penns Mill Lane when he heard the shouts of the men. As might be expected of a person of his rank, he came into the field to take charge of the situation until Mr Webster arrived. The factory men, who were unlettered but highly skilled, well used to working with their hands and to solving engineering problems, probably muttered under their breath and exchanged looks, but they were respectful and let him have his way.

When Simmons returned with the rake he threw it in twice with no success but shortly before eight o'clock, on the third attempt, it caught. Slowly a woman's corpse wearing a pink frock and red spencer (a short, fitted jacket) was dragged to the water's edge. Her face was muddied and blood leaked from the right nostril. Some of the men recognised her as Mary Ashford. William Lavell must have been particularly shocked. He had danced with her just a few hours previously at a Whitsuntide party at Tyburn House, a coaching inn not far away on the Chester Road.

Mary was a friendly, good-hearted girl, only twenty years old, well known locally and well liked for her engaging manner and pleasing appearance. Her family had lived in the area for generations and her parents currently lived near the Cross Keys in Erdington. The family was, in the phrase often used by people of superior social standing, poor but honest, as if the natural default for indigence was dishonesty. Mary was the third of eight or nine children of Ann Coleman and Thomas Ashford and was baptised like her siblings at the church of St Peter and St Paul in Aston, where her parents had married in 1791, there being at that time no church in Erdington itself. Thomas was somewhat feckless and the family had not prospered. Despite this, Mary had apparently had some schooling, paid for by Mrs Tysall, a middle-class woman who had employed her mother. In her teens, after a few years working at the Swan public house, Mary was employed as a live-in servant to her uncle John Coleman, a small farmer at Langley Heath, three miles away. Twice a week she would walk into Birmingham to sell his farm produce at the market, which was then situated between Nelson's statue and Union Street. Her usual spot was by the Castle Inn.

About an hour after the alarm was first raised, Joseph Webster, the owner of Penns Mill, arrived at the pit, a jacket thrown hastily over his nightgown, just as Mary's sodden body was being pulled out of the water. He sent two men back to the Mill to fetch a door that was off its hinges to act as a stretcher and another to alert William Bedford, the local magistrate, who lived at Birches Green to the south of Erdington.

News of the drowning spread fast and some of the villagers rushed up Bell Lane to see what was happening. We do not know whether Mary's parents were among them but in old age her brother William remembered being there soon after her body was recovered. He must have been a forlorn sight, sandy-haired and blue-eyed and slight of build like his sister, standing in shock and grief.

With so many people about in the harrowed field, Lavell and Bird tried their best to keep the footmarks safe. There was no doubt in their minds that a crime, possibly more than one, had been committed and they knew that these marks would be crucial evidence in a future trial. While they did this, William Twamley set off for Tyburn House. He wanted to find out from

5

Daniel Clarke, the landlord, who had been with Mary the previous night at the dance and who had walked home with her.

After Mary's body had been placed on the door, with her belongings alongside, it was carried to William Lavell's cottage, where his wife Fanny was asked to wash it in preparation for an autopsy by a surgeon. Joseph Webster went on to his home, Penns Hall, to dress and came back to the field an hour later, when Lavell and Bird showed him the single footmark on the bank of the pit. Lavell said he thought it looked as if the man had braced himself at the top of the slope in order to throw Mary into the water. After this, Lavell went to issue more warnings to the people in the field not to damage the footmarks and Bird went back to the footpath by Penns Lane. Here, in the heavily dew-laden grass near a tree, he noticed the impression of a body, arms and legs extended. The 'lake of blood' lay at the bottom of this human shape and now he saw that there was another, smaller, bloodstain in the centre. There were also deeper marks in the grass where it looked as if a person's knees and the toes of a man's shoes might have pressed into the earth.

Erdington is seven miles to the north east of the centre of Birmingham. Sutton Coldfield lies three miles or so to the north and Witton to the west. In 1817 it was a small hamlet of humble cottages, pubs and a workhouse (the public library now stands on the spot), where all the families knew each other. The countryside around it was neither beautiful nor especially bounteous — the land was so poor and sandy that people struggled to eke a living from it — but it managed to support a number of market gardens and small farms.

Just under two miles to the north-east of the village was Penns Mill, a huge complex consisting of a mansion, farm and wire factory, which had been owned for three generations by the Webster family. The pit to the south of Penns Mill Lane where Mary was found was a source of marl, which is often used for fertiliser but also to thicken wire drawing lubricants, but it was at that time obsolete; whether that was because it had exhausted its supply or because there were fewer orders is not known. In 1817 Penns Mill was in the middle of a financial crisis: huge losses and bad debts meant short hours for the workers.

One of the reasons Penns Mill was struggling to survive was the severe downturn in demand that came with the end of the Napoleonic Wars in 1815. During the hostilities Bonaparte had banned European trade with Britain, cutting off supplies of German piano wire. Penns began to fill the gap and also produced kitchen equipment and items used in textile manufacture such as needles and cards and pig and hog rings. One of the unfortunate aspects of peace was renewed competition in trade.

It was the same story across the country and, as productivity and wages fell, the mood of the country sank. Even the weather seemed to bring ill fortune. The previous year – known as 'the year without a summer' – had been so bad that the harvest had failed, bringing sharp rises in the price of food. Peppered across the land were black holes of need and suffering, where the poorest were forced to beg or steal. In some towns they were more inclined to assemble, protest and riot.

Nevertheless, life in Erdington, with its triangular hierarchy – labouring poor at the bottom, middling class, professionals and gentry at the top – was no different from any other settlement in Britain. It was a stable community and, apart from the steady encroachment of the city, change took place at a slow pace, mostly unnoticed.

Unnoticed or not, there was a new consciousness afoot. Ideas about human rights unleashed in the French and the American Revolutions refused to die. Radicals, agitators and reformers pressed for political change; some supported universal suffrage (although almost none included women in that demand). Sometimes frustration spilled over into violence. In London, where sporadic civic disturbance was a fact of life, there was a new tenor to the protests, which terrified the government. In December 1816 during what became known as the Spa Fields riots, the firebrand Radical James Watson set off for the Tower of London carrying a revolutionary tricolour and a gunsmith's shop on Snow Hill was looted. Lord Liverpool's Tory government was convinced that a widescale revolt was imminent. Those fears came to a head on 22 January: first, a band of Radicals bearing a petition of half a million signatures asking for electoral reform headed for Parliament; then the window of the carriage containing the Prince Regent was shattered by a missile. It suited the government to dress this up as an attempt on the life of the Prince, an excuse to trigger the Gagging Acts: the suspension of the Habeas Corpus Act, the ancient requirement to produce a person detained by the authorities in a court of law, and the Seditious Meetings Act, which forbade all meetings of more than fifty people which had been called 'for the purpose...of deliberating upon any grievance, in church or state.'

Into this repressive political arena stepped the spinners and weavers of Lancashire and Yorkshire who met at St Peter's Fields near Manchester on 10 March intending to walk to London to appeal for help from the Regent, naïvely assuming that, as Head of State, he would want to alleviate their distress. They were slowly starving, the result of fewer orders and fierce competition from the factory system. Equipped for the long journey with bedrolls strapped to their shoulders, they were soon dubbed the Blanketeers.

This was not a revolution, and the leaders were careful to comply with the laws on illegal assembly by setting off in groups of ten or so. These precautions were useless. Soldiers and constables were sent after them and near Stockport hundreds were arrested, dozens were cut with sabres, and one man was shot dead. Understandably, the protest fizzled out, with most of the marchers abandoning it before even reaching Derbyshire.

Like the Blanketeers, George Jackson, who found Mary's belongings by the pit, had been rendered redundant by the change in demand for his skills: he had worked as a gun borer, but he was now reduced to labouring on the roads, which meant that every morning he walked over seven miles from his home in a poor district in the centre of Birmingham to Newhall just outside Sutton Coldfield. His route would have taken him through the parish of Aston, past the corn mill and the paper mill with its steam-driven engine, skirting Aston Park, and on by the church of St Peter and St Paul. Along the way he would have routinely greeted other early risers: labourers and farmers, milkmen and women, drovers, bargees, carters, pedlars, all part of the massive human machine supplying Birmingham, still then designated a town although it was in reality a big, dirty, noisy city.

Despite the construction of Matthew Boulton's Soho Foundry in 1796, which came to symbolise a new era in which heavy engineering and manufacturing rivalled the trade in household articles and trinkets that the town was known for, industry in Birmingham was still decentralised into small independent and domestic workshops. Nevertheless, it was a busy realm of canals, coal, steam, iron and steel, smuts and noise, home to 100,000 people, and energetically spreading beyond its barely defined boundaries into the countryside.

The fact that Mr Webster ordered Mary's body to be taken to Fanny Lavell suggests that she had experience in 'rendering the last offices'. This task usually fell to women, often to the local midwife, so it is possible that Fanny had that role too. Fanny, aged thirty-nine and newly married to William Lavell, a widower with children, probably knew Mary. Her husband had danced with her at Tyburn House the previous evening, so the Lavells may have been family friends. How it felt suddenly to receive the corpse of this young woman cannot be imagined, but these were hard-working folk, not given and not able to indulge in introspection or fuss. Where there was work to be done, they got on with it.

Shortly afterwards one of Webster's men came back for the shoes. They were wanted back at the field so that they could be compared with the footmarks in the harrowed field. After that Fanny set to work preparing

Mary's body but soon realised that she needed an extra pair of hands. The task of taking off the clothes was not easy. Although Mary was only five feet four (1.6m) and of slender build, she was wearing several layers: spencer, gown, shift (underdress), petticoat and stays, as well as detachable pockets, all of them wet. Fanny must have sent one of the children for her friend Mary Smith, who arrived at the cottage at half past ten.

The women had managed to remove the red spencer when Mr Webster stopped by the cottage. Fanny and Mary Smith may have pointed out to him the black marks on Mary's arms, just above the elbow, which looked like the fingers of a man's hand. Once Webster had gone, Fanny and Mary started to undo the ties on the frock and shift, but where the knots were too difficult they had to rip the clothes. When they took off Mary's pink dress they found a large stain of watery blood and soil on the seat, which had gone through to the petticoat, and a six-inch tear at the bottom of the shift. There were also some stains which they thought might be blood on Mary's thick worsted black stockings, which she wore gartered under the knee, but they were difficult to make out. There was a lot of blood between the thighs. Although they suspected that Mary had been 'violated' it was also clear that, despite not wearing a cloth or rag, she had been menstruating when she died.

As they began to wash the upper surface of the body and the face, blood flowed out of Mary's right eye and down the side of her cheek. Mary Smith remarked to Fanny that she thought the body was not yet cold to the touch. After this, following Mr Webster's instructions, they replaced the clothes as well as they could and awaited the arrival of the surgeons.

Although most crimes were solved by witness testimony or the confession of the perpetrator, most people understood that crime scenes could point to the culprit. William Lavell and Joseph Bird would have been familiar with the sensational story of the poisoning murder of twenty-year-old Sir Theodosius Boughton in 1780 at Little Lawton, only thirty miles from Erdington, and how evidence alone had hanged his brother-in-law at Warwick. Theodosius, a dissolute young man who was being treated for syphilis, would have come in to his fortune if he had lived to be twenty-one, but his death meant that most of the estate would go to his sister and thus to her husband, John Donnellan. The case against Donnellan was entirely circumstantial.

Theodosius was in the habit of putting his medicine on the chimney-piece of his dressing-room so that he would be sure to see it and remember to take it. One evening after returning from a spot of night fishing, he asked his mother to wake him the next morning so that he could take his medicine, and then went upstairs to bed. At seven the next day, she found him very ill, so she did the logical thing and gave him the medicine. She noticed that it smelled and tasted awful, 'like bitter almonds'. Theodosius struggled to keep the draught down and made alarming rattling and gurgling noises. Later he had convulsions, with his eyes staring at the ceiling, his teeth clenched and foam running out of his mouth. His mother sent for a doctor but in the meantime Donnellan arrived and started rinsing the medicine bottle out. When Lady Boughton said, 'What are you at? You should not meddle with the bottle,' he snatched up the other and rinsed it too. At his trial, Donnellan blamed Lady Boughton, the footman, the apothecary and Theodosius himself but was convicted and went to the gallows protesting his innocence.

There was also another more recent, and even more local, case which had weird parallels with Mary's death. On 10 October 1815, Ann Smith, a servant at Over Whitacre, went missing just before she was due to move to a new employer's place. She had asked Isaac Brindley, a fellow servant, to carry her box to a friend's house for safekeeping while she took a jug of barm (used to leaven bread) to a neighbour. She never returned. The following morning her shoe was spotted near a water-filled pit. The chaff and wheat nearby had been trodden down and the barm had been spilt into the ground. Ann's body, bearing black marks and abrasions on the throat and under the ears, was soon afterwards fished out of the pit. The truth was revealed in the impressions found in the mud: a patch set sideways on the knee of a man's corduroy breeches and the heel of a shoe. When Brindley was brought to the scene, he was made to kneel into the mould. At his trial at Warwick in April 1816 a local tailor gave his expert opinion that his breeches were an exact match. Brindley, who had no alibi, was hanged.

Four years previously, the importance of footmarks in achieving justice had been demonstrated in the 1812 murder of Joseph Mycock by his brother Benjamin at Ilam in Staffordshire. Joseph had been sitting by the fire while his wife was at the spinning wheel when a shot was fired through the window. He was killed instantly. The only clue to the identity of the killer was a footmark discovered a few yards from the window. The following day, Benjamin, who had previously worked as a servant for his brother but left after a disagreement, was asked to fetch Mrs Mycock's brother and left his shoes in the kitchen. Mrs Mycock and her daughter took it upon themselves to compare them with the footmark, particularly noticing the two large nails in the front of the heel and a smaller nail between them. Benjamin was convicted at the Stafford assizes and hanged on 18 March, having confessed his guilt.

Chapter 2

Investigation

When Mary's white shoes were returned to Lavell and Bird, they were compared with the woman's footmarks in the harrowed field. There was a bump under the toe of each shoe and a corresponding dent was found in the footmarks. Lavell also discovered a line of the man's footprints running diagonally across the harrowed field, at right angles to the footpath, heading towards a stile in the bottom right-hand corner.

It was about ten o'clock when William Bedford arrived. This 62-year-old Birmingham attorney, born in Droitwich, Worcestershire, was a Deputy Lieutenant and magistrate for the counties of Warwick and Stafford. He had been in the law almost all his life. At seventeen he had been articled to John Dutton, a Worcester solicitor, and thereafter pursued a career in Birmingham, living and working out of premises at 51, New Street. In 1815, when he and his wife Lydia Riland, with whom he had three daughters and a son, moved to a big house at Birches Green, he gave up the day-to-day running of his legal practice and handed it over to his nephew, John Yeend Bedford.

Mr Webster showed Mr Bedford the single footmark by the pit and the blood in the clover field and described how Lavell and Bird had matched Mary's shoes to the woman's footprints in the harrowed field. Then the weather broke and it began to rain (how heavily was a source of contention later), so Bedford suggested that the footmarks be protected with boards and Webster sent a man up to the Mill to fetch some. The footmarks near the dry pit in the harrowed field were covered, two of the man's and one of the woman's, the site chosen because there were plenty of the man's footmarks there, and the owner of these had yet to be identified.

If Mary's parents were at the pit William Bedford would surely have talked to them there. Otherwise, he must have called on them at their house near the Cross Keys in Erdington. Perhaps it was from them that he learned that Mary had gone to the Whitsun dance with her friend Hannah Cox, who worked as a live-out servant to Mr Machin at Erdington Green, and that Hannah would be able to tell him more about what had happened the previous evening.

William Twamley meanwhile was questioning Daniel Clarke, the landlord of Tyburn House, who told him that Mary had left the dance at around midnight in company with a young bricklayer from Castle Bromwich called Abraham Thornton, and offered to ride out to find him. This was easily done; Clarke encountered Thornton only half a mile away nonchalantly riding a pony coming the other way.

'What is become of the young woman that went away with you from my place last night?' asked Clarke.

Thornton made no reply, so Clarke told him Mary had been found murdered.

'Murdered!'

'Yes, murdered,' said Clarke.

'Why, I was with her until four in the morning!'

When Clarke suggested he ride back with him to Tyburn to 'clear himself' he readily agreed. It was a strange journey. They did not mention Mary at all but talked in a desultory fashion about things they saw along the way and farming matters. Thornton asked no questions about Mary and how she died. When they got to the inn, he put his pony in the stable and said he would walk over to Sutton Coldfield – he was probably intending to call on Edward Sadler, the family solicitor – but first he would go into the pub to get something to eat and drink.

During this interlude Abraham Thornton must have mulled over his situation, which was serious and could become terrible. If he was charged and convicted of murder, he would almost certainly be hanged. However, any meditation on the future was soon interrupted by the arrival of Thomas Dales, an assistant constable from Birmingham sent for by Mr Bedford. Within minutes he had arrested Thornton. It was probably at this point that Abraham Thornton sent a messenger for Edward Sadler.

Thomas Dales started to question Thornton and co-opted as a special constable a man who just happened to be in the pub at the time – William Bedson, who worked for Mr Webster at the wire drawing factory, had no relation to the case and no experience of police work. Dales was more used to nabbing petty criminals in the slums of Birmingham than interrogating men suspected of murdering young women and may have had his own reasons for questioning Thornton without Bedford being present, sensing that an opportunity was before him. It was certainly the start of an irregular relationship between the two of them. No record was made of their conversation and Dales later claimed that although they 'were all talking together for some time' it was about 'nothing in particular'. Then Thornton's attorney Mr Sadler arrived at Tyburn House. He seems to have instantly got the measure of Dales, and later disparaged him as 'a runner or thieftaker' who would 'say and swear anything.'

Edward Sadler, aged fifty-nine, was in many ways a typical country attorney. His routine business for the Thorntons was likely to have been property settlements, neighbour disputes, marriage contracts and wills. Although he denied it later, Sadler may have dug Thornton out of scrapes in the past; his young client was rumoured to have been the cause of constant worry to his father, certainly had a reputation for laddishness and was given to boasting and lewd talk. A potential charge of murder, however, was on a different scale from anything that Sadler had previously had to deal with.

Thornton's father, also called Abraham, and mother Sarah (née Hyde) lived in a solid and comfortable farmhouse in its own grounds at Shard End in Castle Bromwich, just over four miles to the south-east of Erdington. While not wealthy, the family were able to afford to keep three servants. Thornton senior was an utterly respectable householder, qualified to serve on juries, and also worked as a steward for land owned by Lord Bradford. The Thorntons had two children. Their daughter Mary was married to Charles Allen Lines, a farmer, but Abraham, aged twenty-four, still lived at home and worked with his father as a bricklayer. Of medium height (five feet seven or 1.7m), young Thornton was exceptionally broad and beefy, with a thick neck and tree-trunk legs, and had dark hair and the beginnings of a double chin. To hide a balding pate, he resolutely combed his hair forward.

Thomas Dales decided it was time to usher the suspect, accompanied by his lawyer and William Bedson, to an upstairs room in order to inspect his clothing. He asked Thornton to unbutton his breeches and found that his shirt tails and the inside part of his breeches, which were made of beige corduroy, were stained with dirt and blood and there were heavy bloodstains on one cuff of his shirt. Dales asked him how that had happened and Thornton told him that he had been 'concerned with a girl' but that it had been with her consent. The extent of the soiling was not officially recorded but it is telling that Bedson chipped in and asked him why there was so much blood. Thornton replied that Mary had warned him that she was not 'fit' (meaning that she had her period) and that he had told her it 'didn't matter', adding that he knew nothing about her murder.

William Bedford arrived at Tyburn House at around eleven, having ridden there directly from his interview with Mary's friend Hannah Cox. It is likely that news that Mary's body had been found in the pit had reached Hannah before Mr Bedford came to her house but even so she must have been in a state of profound distress during the interview. She and Mary had known each other since childhood; they were 'like sisters' she told Bedford. Nevertheless, Hannah managed to give the magistrate a coherent account of the previous night and early morning.

At about ten on Whit Monday morning, Mary, wearing a pink dress, red spencer, half-boots and a straw bonnet, had called for Hannah at her employer Mr Machin's house. Then she and Mary nipped across the way to Hannah's mother Mrs Butler's small cottage, where Mary left the clothes she was intending to wear to the party that evening: a white muslin frock with an underdress, dimity (a cotton fabric with stripes or checks) petticoat, white spencer and white stockings. She asked Hannah to collect her new white shoes from the Erdington shoemaker, and set out for Birmingham market. At six o'clock she returned and the girls got ready for the dance, leaving for Tyburn House between seven and eight and walking the two miles up Bell Lane, then via Holly Lane to Chester Road. In answer to Bedford's direct question about Mary's morals, Hannah was adamant that Mary had been an 'honest' girl, meaning that she was chaste and did not allow anyone to take 'liberties' with her.

The Tyburn was officially called the Three Tuns, but earned its grim nickname from its location on the Tyburn Road, thought to have once been a place of execution and named after the old gallows-place in London. A large flat-fronted three-storey building put up nearly a hundred years before, with snugs and bars, rooms, stables and an annexe, where the party was held, it did excellent business because it sat on the turnpike road near the bridge over the Birmingham and Fazeley canal.

The girls separated during the evening, Mary spending most of the evening downstairs with the music and Hannah upstairs talking to her sister, only going down to the dance for fifteen minutes or so towards the end. At around midnight, she sought Mary out and told her it was time to go. Mary replied that she would not be long, and at this Hannah went to sit on the bridge with her sweetheart, Benjamin Carter. Eventually, fed up with waiting, she sent Benjamin back in to chivvy Mary along and fifteen minutes later Mary emerged accompanied by Abraham Thornton. The four of them started walking along the Chester Road towards the junction with Bell Lane, where Mary's maternal grandfather William Coleman lived. Mary was intending to stay the night at his house. After a little way, Benjamin Carter turned around and went back to the pub to collect something but caught up with the others at the Old Cuckoo, another public house, just before Hannah took the left-hand turning to Erdington, leaving Benjamin, Mary and Thornton to walk the remaining few hundred yards to the crossroads. Benjamin walked on ahead.

The next time Hannah saw Mary it was 4.40am by her mother's clock, when Mary called up at the window asking to be let in. She was in a hurry and quickly changed back into her working clothes: the pink dress, the red spencer and the black stockings (she kept on her white shoes). She told Hannah she had spent the night — which would have been only a matter of a few hours — at her grandfather's and that Thornton had gone home. Then she bundled up her party clothes and half-boots, tucked a handkerchief around her neck and into her bosom, and took up her bonnet. She asked her friend if she would come over to Langley Heath to see her the next day and after giving her hair a quick comb, said 'Don't I look like a rake!', laughed and left.

At Tyburn House William Bedford opened the official examination of Abraham Thornton by saying that he hoped he would be able to clear himself. It was more an admonition than a real desire; he had no doubt that the man in front of him was the culprit. Bedford was under no formal obligation to warn Thornton about self-incrimination but as Thornton was protected by the presence of his attorney, who would have guided him through the interview, advising him on what to say and when to be quiet, he was not disadvantaged. Although the interview was nominally voluntary it was important to get the resulting statement right. As Sadler predicted, it would come to form the basis of Thornton's defence.

Thornton's account of the evening matched Hannah's, at least concerning the walk along the Chester Road and Mary's return to Mrs Butler's to change her clothes. He told Bedford that he had arrived at the Tyburn at six o'clock. At the party, he had danced with Daniel Clark's daughter but — and this was odd considering that the party ended less than twenty-four hours previously and he said he was sober at the end of it — he could not recall if he had danced with Mary. At around midnight he, Mary, Benjamin Carter and Hannah Cox had begun walking down the turnpike road. Hannah and Benjamin had gone their separate ways and he and Mary had reached her grandfather's house at the crossroads, but then walked 200 yards up Bell Lane towards Penns Mill Lane, turned right into a foredrove (a wide, grassy lane) and from there went through four or five fields. Mary had lied to her friend, he said. She did not stop at her grandfather's for the night, or indeed at all. She had been with him.

Did you stray from the footpath? asked Bedford. He was thinking of the footmarks around the top of the harrowed field. No, said Thornton, and added that after they came out of the foredrove, at around three in the morning, he and Mary stood by a stile at the entrance when a man in a brown jacket came by and wished them good morning. Mary said she did not know whether she knew him or not but she thought he had been at the dance at Tyburn (as indeed he had). Later, he and Mary walked towards Erdington, but while Thornton stopped to relieve himself in a field, Mary went on ahead to Mrs Butler's.

Thornton told Bedford that after he emerged from the field, he followed Mary down to Erdington Green and waited there for her. Here Bedford tried a trick question on Thornton in order to catch him out in a lie. Bedford knew that Mary had been at Mrs Butler's cottage to change her clothes. 'Did you see Mary leave Mr Machin's house?' he asked. 'Yes,' said Thornton. 'And what was she wearing?' 'The clothes she wore at the party,' said Thornton. 'The white dress.' If Thornton had really been at Erdington Green he would have seen that Mary was wearing a pink frock and that she did not emerge from Mr Machin's house but from Mrs Butler's.

Why, then, did the final version of Thornton's statement include a completely different version of events at Erdington Green, in which Thornton waited for Mary on the green for five minutes, got bored when she did not appear, and at around 4.10am started for home, not having seen Mary at all? Did Sadler, sensing that Bedford was asking leading questions, encourage his client to backtrack? Or did Bedford realise that whether or not Thornton claimed to have seen Mary come out of the house would not help a future case against him? What he needed was evidence that placed Thornton in the harrowed field after Mary left Mrs Butler's. All the parties were acutely aware from the beginning that timings and distances would be crucial in the investigation and to the success of any prosecution.

Thornton said he saw or was seen by several people on his journey home: a husband and wife who were milking at John Holden's farm to the south of Erdington; Holden's son, who was herding cows; and John Heydon, a personal friend of his, a gamekeeper, of whom he asked the time and stayed for a chat. When he got home, he said, he changed his coat and hat and although his shoes were wet from walking through fields, he kept them on.

While a fair copy of Thornton's statement was prepared (it was likely that a clerk from the New Street office had been sent for to do this) Bedford thought to take a look at Thornton's clothes. Dales had not told him that Thornton had already disclosed that he had had sex with Mary, which invites the suspicion that he was hoping that Bedford would not ask to inspect Thornton's person himself. When Thornton unbuttoned his breeches, Bedford would have been surprised to see his shirt and breeches covered with blood and dirt. Thornton said hastily, 'I have had connection with the girl but it was with her consent.' This crucial piece of information, which Dales should have told Bedford before he started the interrogation, was entirely absent from Thornton's statement. Why was it not added? Sadler may have advised Thornton not to sign a statement that included it, or Bedford may have felt that he had enough against Thornton without the need to further distress Mary's family.

It is difficult for us now to appreciate the impact on Bedford of Thornton's revelation that he had had sex with a young unmarried woman who had a reputation for chastity. He had just interviewed Mary's friend Hannah, who had told him that her friend was an honest girl, and yet here was Abraham Thornton alleging the complete opposite: that within hours of meeting him, she had opened her legs, at night, in the open air — that she had behaved, in other words, like a common prostitute. Bedford was incredulous and revolted. He was interviewing a libertine, a man who led good women astray and whose aim was not their courtship but their conquest. Thornton was a disgusting would-be Don Juan aping the morals of the degenerate upper classes rather than aspiring to the solid values of the middle-class.

Bedford's fellow magistrate Francis Beynon Hacket was the next to arrive at Tyburn, and together they made the decision that there was enough evidence to commit Thornton for trial. They ordered Dales to take him to the lock-up known as Brownell's Hole, the dank basement of a public house in Bordesley, four miles from Erdington.

Lavell and Bird had walked over from the field to Tyburn House and were asking for Thornton's shoes. They wanted to compare them to the marks in the field. William Ashford, Mary's older brother, had also arrived at Tyburn, no doubt wanting to catch sight of the brute suspected of raping and murdering his sister.

Chapter 3

Post-mortem

In the days before railway schedules imposed uniformity, time was not a fixed concept, especially in the countryside. There were essentially three types of time: true time, calculated from a longitudinal position and the sun; conventional time, which might be signalled by a church clock or by a timepiece belonging to a trusted person; all the rest was estimated time. There were often significant variations in conventional time from village to village and an individual timepiece might be fast or slow, or wind down and be re-set by guessing. Some people might keep their clock fast, to fool themselves into getting up in time for work; others might fear upsetting established routines by correcting a clock that had been wrong for years. Webster and Twamley, who took it upon themselves to check the clocks of the witnesses, said they habitually set their own pocket watches to 'Birmingham time'. How fast or slow they were after they did that, we do not know.

Hannah Cox had told Mr Bedford that when Mary came to her mother's house to change her clothes she had glanced at the clock — it showed 4.40am — and that Mary left shortly after the clock struck five. A short time after that conversation, in the field, Mr Webster set his watch by his brother-in-law John William Crompton's and went over to measure Mrs Butler's clock. He calculated that it was forty-one minutes fast, which meant that, by their estimation, Mary had left Mrs Butler's at approximately 4.20am.

Later, while they were at Tyburn, the four gentlemen, William Bedford, Joseph Webster, John William Crompton and William Twamley, agreed that they needed to urgently address the issue of Thornton's alibi. He had mentioned that several people had seen him on his journey home. It was essential to identify them and to verify the timings of those sightings.

William Twamley rode off to John Holden's farm, where Abraham Thornton alleged he was seen by Holden's son and the milk people. He found that Holden's clock showed exactly the same time as his own pocket watch. Then he rode into Birmingham to measure his time against St Martin's church. There was only a minute and a half difference.

Joseph Webster and John William Crompton went to Castle Bromwich to see John Rotton. Thornton had said that Rotton's gamekeeper John Heydon had talked to him for fifteen minutes and told him the time. Heydon explained to Webster that he had his own watch, which he set by Rotton's stable clock. After the clock had struck five, he said, he let down the floodgates near the mill (owned by Zachariah Twamley, a relative of William Twamley's), took up his eel nets, retrieved a fish and was beginning to clean up, all of which would have taken ten or fifteen minutes. It was at this point that he saw Thornton. Webster assessed the stable clock as fifteen minutes faster than his own watch, which meant that Heydon's conversation with Thornton must have occurred just before five o'clock.

Webster understood immediately that there was a problem. If Mary left Mrs Butler's at 4.20 and took twenty minutes to walk from Erdington Green to the fatal field, she would have arrived at around 4.40. Thornton would have had about fifteen minutes to rape her and toss her body into the pit, arrange her belongings and get himself to Twamley's mill by five o'clock. Was that possible?

William Twamley certainly did not think so. On their ride to Castle Bromwich it became clear that Joseph Webster had set his mind against considering any other scenarios but murder by Thornton. For his part, Twamley was increasingly convinced that it was a physical impossibility for Thornton to be at the pit at the time Mary died. In addition, Thornton had freely admitted that he had had 'connection' with her. The girl was apparently willing and sexual intercourse, even if illicit, was not a crime.

William Twamley lived at Newhall Mill, three miles from Castle Bromwich, and his relative Zachariah Twamley was a close neighbour of the Thorntons. While it is true that the population of Castle Bromwich had grown exponentially as industry expanded into the countryside surrounding Birmingham, in 1817 it was home to only about 1,200 souls. It was likely that the Twamleys and Thornton senior knew each other and had done business together. If there was a relationship between them, William Twamley may have felt obliged to give Thornton's son the benefit of the doubt. For now, however, he chose to keep his thoughts to himself. Any doubts about the case would surely be answered at the inquest.

By mid-afternoon almost everyone in Erdington knew that Mary Ashford had been found murdered and that Abraham Thornton had been arrested. Forty years later, a traveller passing through the village that day recalled the atmosphere at a public house where Mary's eight-year-old sister Phoebe was working. The publican discreetly asked the guests not to talk about what had happened within her hearing, 'being anxious to break it to her in the kindest and best manner she was able.'

In the harrowed field, the investigations of the footmarks continued. Bird and Lavell, now in possession of Thornton's shoes, which were made as distinct 'left and rights' rather than the more usual and cheaper 'straights', compared them with the footmarks. The rain had washed into some of the impressions but those that had been protected by the boards were still good. In one right footmark there was a fragment of wood, and after Bird blew it out of the way, he and Lavell saw that towards the toe was the negative of two 'sparrow-bills' (short wedge-shaped headless nails) that exactly matched those on Thornton's right shoe. They felt this was proof enough and now walked back to the Tyburn to hand Thornton's shoes back to Mr Webster, who had returned from Castle Bromwich.

The Coroner, Francis Beynon Hacket, had sent for George Freer, a respected surgeon from the General Hospital in Birmingham, and Richard Horton, a surgeon from Sutton Coldfield, to perform the post-mortem. Their first inspection of Mary's body, at the Lavells' cottage, was cursory — the light was poor and the room cramped, not suitable for a full examination — but they were able to see the blood between Mary's thighs and two deep and fresh cuts to her vagina, which was covered with coagulated blood. They asked Webster to have the body moved to a better location. It was early evening and as the light was fading they made use of their time by going with Webster and William Lavell to the scene of the crime, where Lavell explained his theories about the footmarks in the field and the single footmark by the pit.

The surgeons were not the only ones to visit the place of Mary's death. Earlier, after his client was taken off to Brownell's Hole, Sadler rode over to take a look. In his opinion, the grassy bank under the tree where a human shape was seen and where the presumed rape took place, was hard and dry, and although he accepted that a person had lain on the grass there he could see nothing more than that. As for the large puddle of blood in the footpath nearby, it was scarcely bigger than a tea saucer.

The next day, Wednesday, Bedford and Webster continued their enquiries amongst the inhabitants of Erdington. Several more people had come forward claiming to have seen Mary Ashford and Abraham Thornton in the small hours of Tuesday in places between the Tyburn, Erdington and the foredrove, so Bedford's task now was to interview and take statements from them all, in preparation for the inquest, which would open on Friday at Webster's mansion at Penns Mill.

News about the murder of Mary Ashford had spread. The *Birmingham Commercial Gazette* published a short paragraph giving the barest details. A 'respectable young female' had been found in a pit near Penns Mill in Sutton Coldfield with marks of violence on her body, it reported, and a 'young man of respectable connections' had been taken into custody.

In 1817 Erdington, the start and end points of life did not take place in hospital but out in the world or at home, in bedrooms, parlours and kitchens. These events were seen for what they were: messy, real, human experiences. A cadaver was not necessarily an object of disgust, as it might be now, to be avoided and feared. The dead were a part of life. Just as it was normal to bring dead animals into the kitchen to be defeathered, skinned, butchered and brined, so might a dead human be stripped, washed, dressed and prepared for burial. Perhaps for this reason, the general lack of squeamishness about dead people, it was accepted without fuss by the Lavells and by Abel Taylor, to whose cottage Mary was moved on Wednesday, that her corpse would be in their keeping.

Hosting an autopsy in the parlour, while not usual, was not remarkable either. From time to time it was necessary to use a public house or private home to perform a post-mortem on those who had died through crime, accident or sudden illness. It could be done fairly cleanly. A late-nineteenth-century manual for medical students recommended a 'good firm kitchen table… [or] the coffin lid, or a door removed from its hinges and supported by a couple of chairs'. The windows should be opened and a cloth spread over the table. Wash basins, clean rags, old newspaper, sponges and towels were useful. Freer and Horton would have brought their own portable kits containing a bone saw, scalpels, mallet, chisels, scissors, needles and tweezers.

Freer and Horton delayed the post-mortem until Thursday. We can take a guess that one or other of them had prior commitments or that Bedford wanted to be present and had set aside Wednesday for interviewing witnesses in preparation for the inquest on Friday. Autopsies are best performed as soon after death as possible, but the loss of a day, while regrettable, probably made no difference to the surgeons' conclusions.

The surgeons could only work within the parameters of what they knew. They would have been familiar with *Epitome of Juridical or Forensic Medicine: For the Use of Medical Men, Coroners and Barristers*, published the previous year by another Birmingham man: George Edward Male, who is now considered the 'father' of English medical jurisprudence. His work was a significant advance on Samuel Farr's 1788 *Elements of Medical Jurisprudence*, which itself was a translation from the Latin of Fazelius of Geneva's 1767 *Elemental Medicinae Forensis*. Farr's was the first major manual in English on what we would now call forensic medicine. In many respects, his work was useful and even modern. He advocated that disabled people should be respected as much as the able-bodied and that epilepsy had nothing to do with devils. In other ways, he reflected the world as he knew it: women, the daughters of Eve, were untrustworthy, devious and manipulative and doctors must be on guard for their lies and prevarications.

On the subject of rape, Farr had specific advice for doctors. There were two categories: attempted, when a woman was attacked with great force (male rape was not a recognised concept), and consummated. This last was, for practical purposes, considered possible only when perpetrated on a child. The contemporary view was that except in extraordinary circumstances, it was impossible to rape an adult woman. 'A woman always possesses sufficient power, by drawing back her limbs, and by the force of her hands, to prevent the insertion of the penis into her body, whilst she can keep her resolution entire,' wrote Farr, appending a difficult-to-understand sentence about the woman being able to prevent the penis entering her because 'a lesser resistance can prevail against the motion of any body which acts against the weight,' probably an attempt to convey the idea that 'you cannot thread a moving needle'. A rape would never lead to pregnancy 'for without excitation of lust, or the enjoyment of pleasure in the venereal act [on the part of the woman], no conception can probably take place.' He found injuries during a rape particularly confusing: 'the evacuation of blood from the injured parts, and great swelling and inflammation' that could result from rape could also occur in consensual intercourse. In later editions, the paragraphs about rape stood unedited, although the sentence about 'lesser resistance' was refuted in footnotes.

By the early nineteenth century many aspects of *Elements of Medical Jurisprudence* were seen as outdated (although copies of it would have been retained in medical libraries and surgeons' bookshelves for decades). George Male's new manual was welcomed. The author had high-minded motives — he dedicated his book to Sir Samuel Romilly, a standard bearer for moderate, liberal justice, encouraged surgeons performing autopsies to bear in mind the possibility of 'the same effects being produced by different causes' and reminded his readers that 'where there is the least doubt, be careful that our evidence does not tend to attach suspicion to an innocent person'. 'It is better that many guilty escape, than one innocent man suffer,' he wrote, paraphrasing the great law authority William Blackstone. When it came to rape, however, his *Epitome* was no real advance on Farr's *Elements*.

Male gave only six pages to the subject, in which he outlined the law, erroneously stating that ejaculation had to have occurred for an attack to fall within the legal definition of rape, noting that the age of consent for girls was ten but the age of criminal responsibility for boys was fourteen, conceding that forcing a harlot was a crime (although some of them used 'acrid and stimulating substances' to produce inflammation and fake rape) and ending with a warning about false accusers. Crucially, Male repeated almost word for word Farr's assertion that 'rape cannot be perfected without the exertion of much violence,' although he expanded on Farr's 'extraordinary circumstances', allowing that these might include when 'the woman be subdued by menaces or intoxicated with drugs or spirituous liquors'. In common with all his predecessors, he had nothing at all to say about how to recognise rape-murder.

Freer and Horton had already seen Mary's external injuries. On Thursday, at Abel Taylor's cottage, they had the grim task of opening her body to try to determine what had killed her and whether she had consented to sex with Thornton. We do not know how closely, if at all, they stuck to George Male's recommendations on how to conduct a post-mortem, whether they first looked at her scalp for signs of injury or inside the cranium for fractures, or whether they cracked open her thorax to look at her lungs and heart. It is much more likely that, knowing they should look for evidence of rape and drowning, they started with an incision in her abdomen. In addition, they may have tried to leave her body as intact as they could, out of compassion for her family. Very soon they were able to confirm what Fanny Lavell and Mary Smith had seen, that Mary had been menstruating, and also that the injuries to her 'parts of generation' were caused by 'a foreign body passing through the vagina'.

Even among doctors, knowledge about female bodies was rudimentary. Male surgeons and doctors did not often get an opportunity to examine living women internally; some just reached under their patient's clothes or palpated stomachs and breasts on top of them. There were also strong taboos around menstruation. In any case, no one was quite sure what it was for. The quack doctor Samuel Solomon reflected popular understanding when he wrote that its purpose was to expel an excess of nutrient in the blood. The surgeon John Abernethy, a founder of St Bartholomew's medical school in London and a lecturer at the Royal College of Surgeons, thought it was to 'relieve uterine irritation' and mitigate 'the extreme of sexual desire', enabling women to 'conform to the laws of morality'. The connection between ovulation and the menstrual cycle had yet to be made and it was believed that eggs descended from the ovaries only in response to intercourse.

The surgeons thought that the lacerations to Mary's vagina were recent but that was all they could say — they could not tell exactly when they occurred. Neither could they be sure how much of the bloody mess between Mary's legs was menstrual and how much venous, making it impossible to determine how much she had bled from her injuries, although they thought the blood in the field, including the patch near the tree which appeared to be coagulated, was not menstrual.

The hymen had been 'ruptured on both sides', and Freer and Horton thought that this had happened recently, anything up to ten minutes before death and from this they concluded that Mary had been a virgin before the sexual intercourse, but could not say whether the sex had been consensual or not. Both Farr and Male understood that an intact hymen was not a good indicator of chastity nor a ruptured hymen a sign that sex had taken place and Male rejected the more far-fetched theories that you could determine whether a female had just lost her virginity by looking for 'swelling of the neck, rings around the eyes, the colour of the skin and urine.'

As for cause of death, the question was whether Mary was dead before she went into the pit or had drowned afterwards. In Mary's stomach, Freer and Horton found half a pint of 'thin fluid, chiefly water' and some duckweed and, given the absence of any obvious external injury that would cause death, decided that she been alive when she entered the water. No food was found in the stomach, leading them to think that if Mary had been attacked she would have had little strength to resist.

Chapter 4

Inquest

The inquest on the death of Mary Ashford was held on Friday and Saturday in the ballroom at Penns Hall, the manor house belonging to Joseph Webster. It was more usual to hold inquests in workhouses, hospitals or pubs but because Mary's body was on the Penns estate and a large space was required to accommodate the coroner, a clerk, twelve jurymen, numerous witnesses, the parish officials, Mary's family, the suspect and scores of local people, this was probably the only suitable location. No one saw a conflict of interest between Webster's roles as unofficial investigator of the crime and host of the inquest but Abraham Thornton's attorney, Edward Sadler, was certainly uncomfortable with the choice of venue. He was 'not on terms of friendship' with Webster, and declined to stay overnight at the house, preferring to take up William Twamley's offer of a bed at his house at Newhall.

Sadler's antipathy to Webster was not shared by many. Then aged thirty-seven, the owner of Penns Mill was known as a gentle character and compassionate master. His mettle had been tested early. Aged eight, he had fled across the fields with his siblings, widowed mother, a maid and butler to escape an enraged mob heading for their home. Birmingham at that time was in the grip of a political crisis. Incensed by a banquet held on 14 July 1791 by the Unitarian minister Joseph Priestley and other sympathisers of the French Revolution, a mob of anti-Catholic, anti-nonconformist, anti-reformist rioters, with the connivance of the authorities, targeted dissenting chapels, private houses and businesses. Four days later, having wrought widespread destruction and mayhem and loss of life, they were rampaging through the outskirts of the city, and Penns Hall, owned by the Presbyterian Websters, was in their sights. Only the timely arrival of the 15th Light Dragoons saved it. Thereafter Webster showed himself to be a man who took his responsibilities seriously. At the age of seventeen, assisted by his brother-in-law John William Crompton, he took over the running of the wire drawing factory, which was even then in deep financial trouble, and while still in his twenties was appointed Warden of Sutton Coldfield, which carried with it the duty to act as coroner, and a Low Bailiff of Birmingham.

By modern standards, the organisation of the inquest was hasty, perhaps even chaotic, with no attempt to keep the suspect and the witnesses apart. Thornton, who had been brought from his Bordesley dungeon that morning, was sitting in a room with Thomas Dales, the arresting constable, when his attorney Edward Sadler joined them. A cabinetmaker's apprentice called John Collingwood, who was either working in the house or had come for the inquest, overheard them talking.

'Am I to do what I can for you?' said Sadler.

'You have seen my father?' replied Thornton.

'Yes — be sure and hold fast.'

After Sadler left, Thornton whispered to Dales: 'Sadler says I must hold fast and by God it won't do to own to it.'

When Francis Beynon Hacket, a 33-year-old Cambridge graduate and county magistrate and the current Warden of Sutton Coldfield and thus the Coroner, took his seat the room was full to bursting. Whereas trials at the Assizes were completed swiftly, sometimes in a matter of minutes, with major trials generally taking no longer than a day, it was not unusual for inquests to go into a second day. The remit was not to try Thornton but to look into the cause of Mary's death and to give a verdict. Nevertheless it was in many ways a rehearsal of the trial to come, an early opportunity for both prosecution and defence to test the strength of the evidence. During the course of the proceedings, Sadler, who was allowed to cross-examine witnesses, made copious notes which were later incorporated into a detailed brief for Thornton's barristers.

Between the discovery of Mary's body on Tuesday morning and the opening of the inquest on Friday, Bedford had managed to identify and assemble twenty-five witnesses. Hannah Cox and Benjamin Carter gave evidence about the late-night walk along the Chester Road, with Hannah describing Mary coming to her mother Mrs Butler's house in the early hours to change her clothes, when she had been in a rush but had not seemed in any way distressed; the surgeons Freer and Horton gave evidence of the autopsy and the cause of Mary's death; and four working men who separately saw Mary either going towards Mrs Butler's or coming away from it each stated that she was alone and walking fast. George Jackson told the inquest that after he spotted the bundles, bonnet and shoes by the pit he had gone straight to Lavell's cottage for help. William Lavell and Joseph Bird gave a detailed account of their investigations of the footmarks in the field and the single footmark by the pit as well as the 'lake of blood' and the trail of blood drops.

There was a tense exchange when Bedford asked Lavell whether in his opinion an exhausted female could have thrown herself in the pit and was shut down after Sadler objected to it as an improper question (because it would 'throw no light upon the present enquiry but might leave an impression upon the minds of the jury'). One of the jurymen, who happened to be one of Webster's workmen, later asked the same question, leading Sadler to suspect that Bedford was behind it. It was apparent that Bedford wanted to establish that Mary could not have done so, and that Thornton must have thrown her in.

In his statement to Bedford at the Tyburn, Thornton said that shortly after three o'clock, while he and Mary were standing at the stile at the foredrove, a man in a brown jacket had walked by and greeted them. A 23-year-old tin roller called John Humpage had since come forward and now told the inquest that on his way home to Witton, while he was walking in Penns Mill Lane, he heard people in the fields. He thought he saw through the hedge a woman in a light-coloured gown. Humpage turned into the footpath, where he relieved himself, and the couple walked on some way ahead of him. When he got to the stile at the end of the foredrove he recognised Thornton (he had seen him around the neighbourhood) but not the woman, who was wearing a white dress and spencer. Thornton wished him good morning. Humpage did not see the woman's face because she held her head down. He noticed that she tucked her skirts behind her. This evidence placed Mary in the most northerly point yet; it carried with it the unspoken suggestion that she had been behaving improperly with Thornton in the fields; and it left hanging the question of why she had gone so far in that direction, only to head down to Erdington to change her clothes a short time later.

Several witnesses gave evidence on the whereabouts of Thornton on his way home to Shard End. The milk people at Holden's farm had been traced. William and Martha Jennens told the inquest that Thornton had passed them at about 4.30am. The gamekeeper John Heydon said he chatted to Thornton by the floodgates at Zachariah Twamley's mill at seven or eight minutes past five (or 4.52am or so by Webster's calculation of the true time). This was backed up by John Woodcock, Twamley's miller, who said he had seen Abraham Thornton and Heydon talking as the chapel clock struck five.

Fanny Lavell told the inquest that she had undressed the body, that despite menstruating Mary was not wearing a cloth, that there was a rent in her shift and that her black stockings were not bloody. For Sadler, this was telling. '[It] tends to strengthen the supposition that [the] prisoner had connection with her before she changed her stockings because the stockings she took off when she went to Butler's in the morning were bloody and those were not which they must have been had he had connection with her afterwards.' Mary Smith confirmed that Mary was in 'a bloody state in the lower parts of her body' and that her body was not cold.

James Simmons and Thomas Hiley told the inquest about retrieving Mary's body, and said that 'it appeared that it had been flung into the pit,' because there were no footsteps on the grass there and it was physically impossible for her to have jumped in. Sadler disagreed. 'Certainly, it is possible for a woman to jump or throw herself off a bank six feet high as far as a man could have thrown a woman,' he wrote in his notes, perhaps forgetting that although steep it was not a sheer drop, and Mary would have had to take a running jump in order to reach the water.

When Joseph Webster referred to the human shape in the grass as the 'place the rape was committed' Sadler objected in strong terms. Webster corrected himself — 'the spot where a rape appeared to have been committed' — and went on to describe the footsteps in the harrowed field, the removal of Mary's body and the comings and goings to fetch Mary's shoes from Fanny Lavell and Thornton's shoes from Tyburn. He told the court that he had seen marks looking like the 'strong grasp of a man's hand' on Mary's arms, and that on his visit to Hannah Cox he had measured the disparity between her mother's clock and his timepiece. He had also seen something no one else had thought to mention: there was a distinct impression of dirt on the skirt of Mary's pink gown that looked like the right knee of a person.

According to Sadler, the jury looked at the skirt and could not see it so this part of Webster's deposition was expunged from the record. John Bird, probably a relative of Joseph Bird, disagreed. Sitting amongst the observers at inquest, he saw these marks, which he said looked like they were made by broad corded material similar to Thornton's breeches, and claimed that others, including some of the jurymen, did so too. Bird was an intelligent and observant man who worked as Joseph Webster's trusted production manager (he was later promoted to run another of Webster's factories at Killamarsh in Derbyshire) and his careful notes are preserved in Birmingham Archives. He noted down the state of the clothes presented at the inquest. Mary's white gown had a small stain of blood 'about the size of a thruppenny piece' at the back in the centre and bore no marks of soil. The white stockings were spotted with blood. Mary's pink gown was

28

heavily soiled with dirt and blood, which the pond water had failed to wash out. The petticoat and shift were likewise stained with blood and the shoes were bloody inside and out. He could see no blood on the black stockings, perhaps not surprising since they were made of thick worsted wool and gartered under the knee. Thornton's shirt had blood on the front and there was blood on the outside of his breeches 'where [he] wiped his bloody hand after he had completed his lustful passion' and on the inside. There were no soil marks on the knees of the breeches, which Bird took as proof that Mary's gown had been under them while she was being raped.

Edward Sadler and William Bedford clashed bitterly when Bedford alleged that Thornton had told him that he had seen Mary emerge from Mr Machin's house in her party dress. 'Why did you not include this in Thornton's statement?' demanded Sadler. Bedford's explanation, that it was an oversight caused by the 'hurry of the moment', was unconvincing and Sadler suspected that Bedford had deliberately manipulated Thornton's statement in other ways — in his notes he complained of 'several alterations' being made to it between the draft and the final version. There was also another point of contention: Thornton's disclosure that he had sex with Mary, made when Bedford inspected his clothes. Bedford claimed that Thornton made his admission only after his statement had been taken and signed. Sadler said it could only have occurred before this, because Thornton was taken away to the dungeon at Bordesley straight after signing the statement.

Why did Sadler care so much about these seemingly small matters? Were they really of great significance when his client was claiming, in any case, that the sex was consensual and at the time of Mary's death he was miles away? Thornton had only a handful of supporters. Almost everyone thought he was guilty and a few villagers would even have been convinced that he had real diabolical powers: the ability to fly, perhaps, or to be in two places at once, for despite rapid advances in science and the promotion of 'rational religion' superstitious beliefs in witches, sprites and devils, persisted, and not just among the poor and uneducated.

In Sadler's opinion, the investigators were biased against Thornton from the start. He believed that Bedford and Webster were 'the prosecutors or rather the persecutors for the investigation.' Their conduct at the inquest was 'disgraceful... as gentlemen and particularly so Mr Bedford as a magistrate' who, he felt, encouraged an atmosphere of prejudice against Thornton that was 'beyond measure great'.

Based on what Thornton had told him in private conversations, Sadler had formulated his own theory for what had happened in the early hours of

Tuesday. It was a sordid tale and his client did not emerge well from it, but it did not make him a murderer. After Hannah went off home on her own and Benjamin Carter went on ahead, Thornton and Mary continued on up to the junction of Chester Road and Bell Lane. Mary had decided, or was persuaded by Thornton, not to stay with her grandfather who lived next to the crossroads, so they walked north to the foredrove and entered the fields. At the tree (where the impression of a person was seen in the grass the following day), Thornton took off his coat and laid it on the grass to prevent Mary's white gown from becoming soiled. They had sexual intercourse, after which Mary urinated near the path. Thornton had told Sadler that he did not notice any 'bloody matter' at the time but this probably accounted for the 'lake of blood' found there.

Then they walked back towards the stile and Mary noticed that the back part of her white gown was bloodstained. At the stile, where they were seen by John Humpage, Mary held her head down in shame at her behaviour and tucked her skirts behind her to hide the stains. She told Thornton she would return to Erdington to change her clothes and collect her bundle and they then walked down Bell Lane past the horsepit to Thomas Greensall's farm, where Thornton went into a field to relieve himself, saying that he would catch up with Mary later. When he got to Erdington Green he waited for her for five minutes, changed his mind and went on home. If Mary did not seem upset when she was with Hannah at Mrs Butler's house it was because she was not. The sex had been entirely consensual. However, her return to the field on her way home to Langley gave her time to reflect. When she saw the blood on the grass near the tree, she was so overwhelmed with regret at her momentary lapse of morals that in despair she made a sudden and dreadful decision to throw herself in the pit.

The inquest verdict, which came late on Saturday evening, was no surprise to anyone: Wilful Murder by Abraham Thornton. The prisoner was committed for trial at the next Warwickshire county assizes in August, but first he was taken, probably by Thomas Dales, to Birmingham Gaol at Moor Street to await transfer to Warwick.

After the inquest, Sadler made his way to William Twamley's house. He was angered and disturbed by Webster's and Bedford's behaviour at the inquest — particularly the question about whether Thornton had seen Mary at Erdington Green and the timing of his disclosure of sex with Mary — so when Joseph Webster called on Twamley that evening he saw an opportunity to give vent his feelings.

'Did you hear any such declaration?' he asked Webster, referring to Thornton's alleged sighting of Mary as she emerged from Mr Machin's house. Webster replied that he knew nothing of it and that did not even hear Bedford give this evidence at the inquest.

'You were out of the room,' said Sadler, showing him his notes.

'I am surprised,' said Webster. 'It was what Bedford and I had been hunting after all week.'

Sadler insinuated that Webster had perjured himself although he glossed this by saying it may have been inadvertent.

The following day, Sunday, as Mary's body was being put into the ground in Sutton Coldfield churchyard, Sadler rode home to contemplate the best strategy for saving his client from the hangman in the face of enemies intent on twisting every fact to suit their story. He could only conclude that a robust response was required.

Chapter 5

Preparations

At his home in Birches Green, William Bedford's anger festered. Sadler's humiliating cross-examination ('Why did you not include in Thornton's statement his assertion that he saw Mary at Erdington Green?') with its imputation that he was incompetent, or even lying, rankled. And now Webster had told him about the bad-tempered conversation he had had with Sadler at William Twamley's house.

A day or two after the inquest, thinking it would be better to catch Thornton while he was in Birmingham Gaol before he was moved eighteen miles away to Warwick, Bedford rode in to the city to confront the cause of all this misery. He entered Thornton's cell as he was at dinner.

'How could you have the impudence to deny what you said?' he demanded.

'I never made any such declaration,' replied Thornton, unfazed.

'But I'll swear it! And how can you eat, knowing what awaits you? You will be hanged and your body will be given to the surgeons for dissection. You have long deserved it for you have cost your own father many a hundred pounds to get you out of scrapes of this kind.'

We have only Sadler's second-hand account of their encounter, which must have come from Thornton himself, so it is difficult to know how much of it was true. Sadler certainly believed it. As a friend of the family and their attorney, he would probably have known about Thornton's 'scrapes' but the brief he later compiled for the barristers, which included a description of this encounter, denied them. He certainly felt sympathy for Thornton's family and he knew that Abraham Thornton senior, who had terminal tuberculosis, was not expected to live long.

Bedford was not Thornton's only visitor at Birmingham Gaol. A family friend, a stonemason called John Davis, brought him supplies of food and drink and stayed to talk. He was surprised by what Thornton told him about what had happened with Mary but for the time being, not wanting to bring trouble to the Thorntons or to himself, said nothing.

PREPARATIONS

Two weeks after Mary's body was pulled out of the marl pit, the rumblings of a revolt started in the tiny village of Pentrich in Derbyshire, thirty-five miles to the north-east of Erdington. A group of two or three hundred stockingers, quarrymen and iron workers armed with pikes and pistols set out to march to Nottingham. William J. Oliver, a government spy, had encouraged their leaders to believe that they would be joining 50,000 other protesters and that together they would storm the Tower of London. Instead, he delivered them into the arms of a regiment of soldiers lying in wait for them. Thirty-five of the would-be revolutionaries were arrested, charged with High Treason and locked up in Derby Gaol.

After the privations of Brownell's Hole and Birmingham Gaol, Thornton would have found conditions at Warwick Gaol reasonably comfortable. The building, which was then barely twenty years old, housed male and female felons and debtors in a series of courtyards overlooked by the turnkey. According to the Unitarian minister William Field, who published a detailed description of it in 1815, the prison was 'light and airy' and the regime, if not benign, was at least acceptable. There were night rooms and day rooms, hot and cold baths, a garden and glazed windows, and leg irons were used only occasionally.

Most of the prisoners shared cells. For a few weeks, Thornton's companion was Omar (or sometimes Homer) Hall, a former banker who had fallen far in fortune and had recently been sentenced to transportation. Born into a prosperous Stafford family and now aged 42, Hall had tried his hand as a draper, coal merchant and tramway developer, but all his ventures had ended in financial ruin. His most spectacular failure was the bank he founded at Stafford, which came to an abrupt end in 1807 after thieves broke in and stole over two thousand pounds in notes. A week later, Hall was declared bankrupt. Suspicion about the break-in, and who was behind it, did not go away and, after another business failure in 1811, Hall left Stafford with his reputation in tatters. He had since led a peripatetic life, ending up, at least once, in prison for debt. In 1817, he was reduced to stealing fowls, for which he was found guilty at Warwick Lent Assizes. His sentence, seven years transportation to New South Wales, was unusually harsh and it is difficult to avoid the suspicion that he was being punished for previous transgressions. While Hall awaited transfer to the prison hulks in London before his onward voyage, Henry Tatnall, the Warwick gaoler, sensibly made use of his skills by ordering him to work as a scribe for illiterate prisoners and had provided him with pen, ink, paper and sealing wax for the purpose.

Thornton and Hall often walked together in the felons' courtyard, swapping notes on their lives and adventures, Hall mentally filing the information Thornton divulged about Mary Ashford. Prisons house the most manipulative people in society and Hall, whose rollercoaster career exposed him as devious and unreliable, was now the owner of secrets about Thornton. He decided that it would do him no good to tell tales on his cellmate — just yet. For now, he was content to watch him carefully. One of Thornton's visitors caught Hall's attention: Thomas Dales, the Birmingham assistant constable, came to the prison to speak to Thornton, and Hall saw the two of them whispering together. After Dales departed, Thornton wanted to use Hall's pen and paper to write a letter but Hall piously refused, saying that the governor forbade it. Eventually, however, he gave in after Thornton convinced him that he would send Hall money after his trial. He seemed to be in no doubt that he would be acquitted.

William Bedford and Edward Sadler both spent the nine weeks before Thornton's trial assiduously gathering evidence. For the defence, Sadler hunted down more witnesses, commissioned a map of the area, visited Slade End to confer with the Thorntons, who would be footing the bill to save their son, chose the barristers and compiled a sixty-two-page brief to instruct them. This remarkable document, annotated with Sadler's observations on the witnesses and an account of the inquest, has survived and reveals his strategy for winning the case. He knew that defending Thornton would be difficult — the 'chain of circumstance [is] very unfavourable,' he wrote — and complained of prejudice against his client. He particularly objected to the numerous songsheets and handbills about Mary's murder already circulating at fairs and markets in the area. The titles of these one-penny 'broadsides' speak of the high emotion surrounding the case: *The Sorrowful Lamentation of Mary Ashford's True Lover (My Mary is murdered! My breast swells with anguish!), Mary Ashford's Tragedy… (Mary Ashford's ghost proclaims the sad tale), The Fancy Lad (When first I came to town) — A New Song on the Ghost of Mary Ashford*. 'A serpent surprised her, the worst of its kind,' went one typical ballad, 'For pity, she cried, but she cried to the wind.' Despite Sadler's fears that 'it will be extremely difficult to select a trial jury whose minds are not previously influenced by these fabricated and malicious publications,' he was absolutely sure that Thornton would be acquitted. His view was that the alibi was unassailable.

William Bedford was just as busy, spending his time marshalling the evidence and briefing the prosecution. Like Sadler, he commissioned a map to present to the court, this one from William Fowler, a land surveyor who had lived in Erdington all his life and therefore knew the area well. Bedford also understood the importance of timings and distances. He was sure that the footmarks in the field would prove that Thornton was the culprit — there were no other suspects.

There seemed no end to the lurid rumours in Erdington about how Mary died. People were saying that Mary's brains had been dashed out, that her head had been almost severed, that her body had been mangled and was found covered in wounds, that a handkerchief was missing and that Thornton had used it to stuff into her mouth during the rape and that Thornton's shirt had been washed before it was produced at the inquest. Sometimes, amid the noise and false stories, information of substance emerged. A new witness was identified, with evidence of Thornton's intention to attack Mary. In the Cross Keys pub one night, Thomas Ashford was talking about his daughter to a young farmer called Joseph Cotterill, who told him that on Whit Monday he had been standing outside the Tyburn with Thornton, John Cooke and a couple of other men when Mary arrived with Hannah.

'What wench is that?' Thornton asked him.

'One of old Ashford's daughters,' he replied.

'She's a nice wench,' said Thornton. 'I remember her from the Swan' (the pub on Erdington Green where Mary had worked as a teenager). 'I've had her sister three times,' he added, meaning Ann, the eldest of the Ashford siblings. 'And I'll have her tonight, if I die for it.'

Later, Cotterill had danced with Mary and asked her if she had a beau, but neither he nor the other men who had heard what Thornton said thought to warn her that he had set his sights on her.

Warwick Gaol, despite its relatively good conditions, held a darker past. Before the gaol was rebuilt, up to fifty-nine prisoners would sleep in a small circular dungeon in the yard, their bodies arranged in a carousel around a central cesspit, so closely packed that they were able to lie only on their sides. Those primitive days were over, thanks to the vociferous objections of prison reformers, but the Hole, as it was known, was not entirely obsolete. When the courts were sitting, the metal grill over the entrance was removed to allow prisoners and their guards to descend a 19-foot (6m) ladder and follow a narrow underground tunnel which emerged in the Shire Hall. Here they would stay until called and escorted up to one of the octagonal courtrooms.

The first day of the Assizes fell on Thursday 7 August, when over a hundred 'unfortunates', most of them poor, ill, damaged or otherwise disadvantaged, followed the route down the Hole, along the tunnel, to one of two courtrooms, where they were placed at the bar to learn at first hand about the unpredictability of Georgian justice. Prosecutors and barristers spoke about them, judges fired questions at them, witnesses denigrated or lied about them and a jury pronounced a verdict on them. If found innocent they were dismissed but if guilty they left the court to return to the holding cells, temporarily, after which it was the turn of the next batch.

The two Assize judges, Mr Justice Clarke and Mr Justice Holroyd, managed to clear most of the cases by half past two. Then the court recessed and they retired to the Judges' Lodge adjacent to Shire Hall for a two-hour break. When the court reconvened, the men, women and children who had the misfortune to be convicted were marched back to the bar in groups of twelve to hear their fate. Most were punished with imprisonment or transportation. Forty-seven were condemned to death.

England's statutes defined over two hundred crimes as felonies, all of them capital offences. Some of them were absurdly trivial and all but a few were connected with the Georgian obsession with property. To steal from a rabbit warren, be in the company of gypsies for a month, cut down trees in an orchard and go about at night with a blackened face were all capital offences and, although no one had been executed for these crimes for years, plenty still 'suffered' for property crimes such as burglary, forgery and fraud. Reformers in the early nineteenth century, exasperated and appalled by the continuing toll of blood at the gallows, invented the term 'the bloody code' for England's criminal laws. By sticking to this cruel and arbitrary system, they said, the justice system betrayed itself as barbaric and its cruelty medieval. No other civilised nation behaved in this way. In any case, the capital sentences handed down amounted to pointless posturing because almost all those condemned to death were later reprieved, as indeed were the forty-seven condemned on the first day of the Warwick Summer Assizes.

Nevertheless, as Thornton waited in his cell on Thursday, now without the companionship of Omar Hall, who had been transferred to London in July, he may have had secret misgivings about his chances of getting off the charges of murder and rape laid against him. 1817 was already proving to be a particularly fatal year for England's felons: seventy-three men and women had been hanged, although only one at Warwick so far. During the Lent Assizes, William Stokes, a 35-year-old gilt toy maker with a wife and six children, had walked through the 'dead room' above the turnkey's lodge at the prison, to the platform erected outside where, after the usual ceremonies and prayers, he was 'turned off' by the hangman. His crime was not even murder, but the passing of fifty-four counterfeit banknotes. The Bank of

36

England was cracking down hard on forgers and was keen to send out a message that the law would punish the crime to the utmost. No such message was required for murderers. They were almost never reprieved. Of the twenty-five people found guilty of murder in 1817, all were hanged.

If Thornton was at all concerned by the possibility of being convicted for murder, he would have had almost no worries about the rape charge. As now, few rape cases reached courts and when they did acquittal rates were high. At the Old Bailey in the fifty years up to 1817, eighty-two per cent of defendants charged with rape were found not guilty. Those few who were convicted were more often than not reprieved from the gallows and sentenced to transportation or imprisonment instead.

In the main, only men who attacked children were hanged. Even this crime was sometimes viewed, if not with sympathy, at least with understanding of the motive. It was a widespread belief that having sex with a virgin would cure syphilis and other venereal diseases. Some got off for other reasons. In April 1817, William Townley was tried at the York Assizes for repeatedly raping his eleven-year-old stepdaughter. A surgeon proved the injuries to the child but Justice Bayley felt that the 'mere story of a child, unconfirmed by other corroborative testimony, would not warrant them to come to a conscientious conclusion of the prisoner's guilt.' In addition, common law held that because a woman on marriage became 'one person' with her husband, she was not generally competent to give evidence against him. To do so would be to incriminate 'herself' (the only exception being in cases where a husband was accused of personal violence against his wife). Townley was acquitted.

In a prosecution for rape there were legal requirements that did not apply to other crimes. The victim had to report a complaint of rape within twenty-four hours and prove, through marks of injury, disordered clothing or eyewitness testimony, that she had been forced and that she had resisted. She could not simply say that she had been cowed into compliance or claim that she had been paralysed with fear. She also had to have cried out. In 1796 eleven-year-old Mary Homewood alleged that David Scott, a dyer, had raped her when she delivered beer to his lodgings from her father's pub in Spitalfields in the east of London. Peter Alley, a seasoned barrister, subjected her to a lengthy and aggressive cross-examination:

Q: Did you cry out when he seized hold of you?

A: Yes.

Q: You cried out when you were standing at the door?

A: Yes.

Q: Did he drag you in from the door when you cried out?

A: No. He told me to put down the beer.

Q: After you cried out?

A: Yes.

Judge: Do you understand what the gentleman says? Did you
    cry out before you put the beer down?

A: No.

Q: Had you put the beer down?

A: He did not offer to touch me before I put down the beer.

Q: He laid you down upon the bench?

A: Yes.

Q: Had you cried out at all before the door was shut?

A: He told me to put it down inside the room.

Q: The room door was then open?

A: Yes.

Q: And he came and laid hold of you?

A: Yes, and shut the door.

Q: Did you cry out before he dragged you to the form [bench]?

A: No.

Q: Then you cried out before the door was shut?

A: Yes.

Perhaps it was the youth of the victim, only a year over the age of consent, that led the jury to convict Scott, who was sentenced to death and hanged at Newgate on 10 November 1817.

The victim also had to prove that she had tried to escape. In a notorious case of 1786, John Motherhill, a poor tailor, was tried for the rape of a 21-year-old woman with learning difficulties. On a dark stormy night in September, Catherine Wade had been dropped off by friends near her Brighton home and was trying to get into the house when Motherhill intimidated her into going with him to a graveyard, where he raped her. She was accused of not resisting or shouting out for help. According to Motherhill's defence barrister, 'He did not take hold of her as she went along North Street, but suffered her to go first, and he followed at some little distance; she did not state any efforts she made to get from him, tho' repeatedly asked the question; there were lights in several of the windows as she went along, but she did not attempt to knock at either doors or windows.'

How the jury viewed Catherine's apparent failure to resist is not known. It appears that it was Motherhill's possible punishment that concerned them more. At the end of the trial at East Grinstead, Surrey, after asking the judge a specific question about the death penalty, the jury conferred for half an hour and acquitted.

It was not unusual for the victim to undergo intimate examination by several medics and to be forced to speak in graphic terms in court about what had happened. In 1797 Jane Bell, aged about fourteen, was attacked by a man as she was locking her mistress's cows in Green Park in London for the night. He hauled her off into the park to Constitution Hill and flung her to the ground where he raped her. At least three men, an apothecary and two surgeons, examined Jane. Mr Winterbotham gave evidence at the Old Bailey:

Q: Did it appear as if the body had been entered for the first time?

A: There was no laceration, no blood, but there appeared to be human semen upon the private parts.

Q: Was the hymen broke?

A: There was no appearance of it.

Q: Did it appear as if she had been entered for the first time?

A: To all appearance.

Q: How should there be that appearance if there was no laceration, and no blood?

A: From the smallness of the parts, and the appearance of violence, I could not suppose she had been a common girl. I cannot say, positively, that it was the first time; it is my opinion, that he had endeavoured to enter, and I observed the semen.

Q: Without supposing her to be a common girl, do you think she might have had any man with her before?

A: No, not in my judgment.

The law at that time was a mish-mash of precedent and practice, with judges sometimes determined to go 'off piste' to create rules. Rape was no different. In practice, some judges required evidence, in virgins at least, that the hymen had been broken (even though this was not a reliable test) and others evidence of penetration and emission. What would be the situation if penetration could be proven but emission occurred outside the body? Or if the victim was too young to be able to describe what had happened? Often these would be prosecuted as attempted rape, a misdemeanour, because the chances of conviction were higher although the punishment was correspondingly light.

For complainants, there was always a risk that the tables would be turned and they would find themselves in the dock. This was especially so where the defendant was of a higher social class. In August 1819, after she was sacked by her master, Samuel Mills, a 48-year-old former army captain and magistrate, fifteen-year-old maidservant Hannah Whitehorn told her mother that the Captain had raped her at his home in Chelsea. He had pulled her into the parlour, plied her with strong drink and forced her upstairs into his bedroom, where he attacked her. Later she suspected that he had given her a sexually transmitted disease. Mills was arrested, taken before a magistrate and remanded to prison. When the case came up at the Old Bailey, he was defended by top barristers John Adolphus and John Barry and Hannah faltered under their fierce cross-examination and inferences that she had been infected before she started working for Mills. The jury conferred briefly and acquitted him. The following year, Mills prosecuted Hannah for perjury and in court claimed that he had dismissed her because she stank. It did not help his case that he could not explain why eight female servants had left his employ in five months or why two of them had made official complaints about him to the police and Hannah was acquitted.

What happened if a woman died in the course of a rape or attempted rape? The aggressor would generally be charged only with rape and not with murder. In his 1799 *Treatise on the Law of Homicide*, Robert Bevill wrote, 'In most cases, the act of committing a rape cannot imply a "compassing or designing to do some body harm"; there is then no probability that it will occasion death or personal injury, and therefore under the above rule it cannot be murder.'

Thornton was arraigned first on a charge of murder. The prosecuting team would not be alleging that Thornton killed Mary during the rape, but that he had made a deliberate decision to drown her afterwards.

Chapter 6

Prosecution

From the start of the trial Thornton appeared to be unconcerned at his situation. He stood at the bar, in his smart black coat and yellow waistcoat, listening intently to the witnesses but completely deadpan, a picture of aloof confidence. Not a shadow of emotion or distress passed over his face.

Friday 8 August would be a long day for him, but longer for the observers of the trial, many of whom treated it more as a spectacle than a serious display of public justice. Crowds had started to assemble in the space in front of the Shire Hall as early as six o'clock and a crush had rapidly formed. By eight, when the High Sheriff, lawyers, jurymen and witnesses started to arrive, the javelin men, the liveried yeomen retained by the Sheriff to escort the judges of assize, struggled to keep people back to allow them into the vestibule.

All ranks were there, from the lowliest of labourers to the most respectable of gentlemen, among them James Amphlett from the *Lichfield Gazette* and a journalist from *The Times*, as well as John Cooper, a printer from Warwick, and numerous shorthand writers. There were no women. Talk of ripped and bloody frocks, lacerations, broken hymens and menses would be too much for their delicate sensibilities, and the authorities had decided that they should not be admitted.

Inside the cramped assize courtroom, Justice Holroyd ordered proceedings to start, and the clerk began to call and swear in the jury. These men were all of the middling sort: respectable farmers, drapers, steelworkers and yeomen, not much different from Abraham Thornton's own father, in fact, who was himself a juryman in Castle Bromwich. Then the accused, who was referred to throughout the trial as the Prisoner, was brought up from the cells and placed at the bar facing the judge.

At nine, the gates outside were finally opened and the public streamed in to find seats in the gallery, where they could look down into the well of the court. We can speculate that Edward Holroyd, the judge's 23-year-old barrister son, was guaranteed a seat or was accommodated on the floor of the court or even on the bench itself. He took copious notes and later claimed that his was the most accurate of the many published accounts that appeared afterwards.

Everyone had eyes only for Thornton, the alleged murderer. What did they see? *The Times*'s man thought he was monstrous — his 'excessive corpulency has swollen his whole figure into a size that rather approaches to deformity,' he wrote. Perhaps he was merely reflecting contemporary wisdom: evil was as evil looked, especially with the benefit of hindsight, or perhaps Thornton, deprived of the strenuous exercise that was part of his job as a bricklayer, had put on weight during his incarceration. Other journalists remarked that he was 'repulsive', while still others found him to be a 'stout, well-looking young man' with a fresh complexion. One thing they all agreed on; the Prisoner did not seem to be at all bothered by proceedings.

The trial was run by an array of Georgian gentlemen whose origins varied from the humble to the solidly middle class. This was a time of social mobility for clever, ambitious boys wanting to get on in the law profession — after all, the Lord Chancellor Lord Eldon was the grandson of a Newcastle water-carrier and broker of coals. The judge who heard the case, George Sowley Holroyd, was the son of a gentleman, but he had known adversity. His father lost a fortune and young George, unable to attend university as a result, was instead articled to a London attorney. He made a good fist of it, becoming a barrister on the Northern circuit and eventually a judge of the King's Bench. As a younger man, he lived on the edge of the radical, or at least the reform, movements. He associated with the great law reformer Samuel Romilly, and his great claim to fame was to appear for the radical Sir Francis Burdett in his suit against Charles Abbott, Speaker of the House of Commons. Now fifty-eight, Holroyd had developed a calm, unruffled manner, and was praised for his clear legal arguments and remarkable memory but not particularly, according to the anonymous author of his obituary in *The Gentleman's Magazine*, for his 'store of wit'. What brains he had he managed well, and he studied hard, but he lacked 'forensic abilities'.

William Bedford had selected some heavy hitters to prosecute the case. Nathaniel Gooding Clarke started life sixty-one years previously as the son of a Norfolk ironmonger. After Caius College, Cambridge, he was admitted to Lincoln's Inn and called to the Bar, later becoming Recorder of Walsall and Chief Justice of Brecon and Carmarthen. At the time he prosecuted Abraham Thornton he was working as a senior counsel on the Midland

Circuit. His colleague, 45-year-old serjeant-at-law John Copley, had an unusual background for a lawyer. Born in Boston, Massachusetts, he was the son of John Singleton Copley, the famous American painter of colonial celebrities. Alfred Thrale Perkins, aged thirty-six, was the junior.

Edward Sadler had chosen two exceptionally astute lawyers to face down the prosecution, both of them, like Clarke, stalwarts of the Midlands Circuit. William Reader, the son of a Coventry wool merchant, had once nursed radical ideas — in his thirties he was a member of the Society for Constitutional Information, which was suppressed by the government for campaigning for parliamentary reform and promoting Thomas Paine's *Rights of Man* which, to the alarm of the authorities, advocated democratic republicanism — but now, aged fifty-eight, he had settled into a solid conservatism. His mental agility was undiminished, however, and he was known for the extraordinary energy he brought to his twin jobs as a barrister for hire and Recorder of Coventry. Alongside Reader stood 42-year-old Henry Revell Reynolds, whose many years' experience in the criminal courts in London and on the Midlands Circuit, brought him a reputation as cool-headed and professional.

For centuries, the purpose of the trial had been to allow the accused personally to answer the charges against him. It was essentially a controlled altercation; a direct confrontation between the victim (the prosecutor) and the defendant. While it was the defendant's opportunity to speak and explain, it was part of the judge's remit to protect the defendant from incriminating himself. The practice of employing defence counsel was slow to grow. From 1696, they were permitted to appear in treason trials and from the 1730s they could do so in felony trials but it took another fifty years for their use to became regarded as unremarkable. Their services were not free and the state was under no obligation to provide them.

The presence of defenders in court contributed to a shift of focus; by the early nineteenth century, the trial was more of an opportunity for the defence to test the strength of the prosecution case than for the defendant to explain himself. Put another way, as the lawyer became the mouthpiece of the defendant, the defendant retreated into silence. Indeed, often the advice of counsel was to say nothing at all, not even in the form of a defence statement, in effect to 'go no comment'.

Thornton's parents paid for his defence and used up their cash reserves to do so. They were lucky to be able to support their son. Those without access to credit but in possession of a little cash might be able to engage a jobbing lawyer to prepare a written defence, to be read out by the judge in court, but the poorest, unable to afford even that, had to rely on their own abilities and act as their own barristers. They could challenge witnesses and were entitled to speak at the end of the trial but in reality, most were too overwhelmed to do anything more than simply deny the charge. Poor William Stokes, the utterer of false banknotes tried at Warwick, was convicted on the word of one of his customers and was able only to state that this person had induced him to commit the crime. When Isaac Brindley, who was accused of murdering Ann Smith (and whose corduroy breeches had made an impression in the mud and in the minds of Lavell and Bird), was called on to make a defence, he replied 'I know nothing of it.' Both Stokes and Brindley went to the gallows.

Thornton was indicted first for the murder of Mary Ashford, to which he pleaded not guilty; the rape charge would be heard after the first case was heard. In his opening address, Nathaniel Gooding Clarke described the murder as 'of the highest enormity... one of the greatest offences that human nature is capable of committing — that of shedding human blood — the innocent blood of a fellow creature' and Mary as 'of unblemished character', the child of 'poor but very honest parents'. He summarised the events and emphasised the extreme violence done to Mary but glided over the difficult issue of the timings.

Nearly all the witnesses for the prosecution had previously appeared at the inquest, and the evidence they gave at Warwick was, in the main, the same. Hannah Cox was the first to stand in the witness box. Under questioning by Serjeant Copley, she told the court about Mary's movements on Whit Monday when she arrived at Mr Machin's in her pink frock, red spencer, black stockings and half-boots; Mary was going to Birmingham market and asked her to pick up the new white shoes from the Erdington shoemaker. Then they had crossed the road to Hannah's mother Mrs Butler's, where she left her party clothes: the white dress, white spencer and white stockings. At six she returned, called on Hannah at Mr Machin's, and afterwards they got ready for the party at Mrs Butler's and walked over to Tyburn House. Hannah said she spent only fifteen minutes in the dancing room and between eleven and twelve o'clock came to tell Mary it was time to go, and that she would wait for her on the bridge thirty yards from the inn. Benjamin Carter was with her, and when Mary did not appear, she sent him in to hurry her up. A few minutes later Mary emerged with Abraham Thornton and the four of them set off down the Chester Road. Thornton and Mary went on ahead, Benjamin Carter and Hannah following, until Carter turned back to the Tyburn. Hannah walked with the others and, shortly after Carter caught up with them, went alone down a road leading to Erdington. A few hours later, Mary woke her by calling up at the window, and she got out of bed to let her in. By her mother's clock it was 4.40am:

Q: (John Singleton Copley, for the prosecution) Did you perceive any agitation or confusion in the person of the deceased?

A: No.

Q: Neither her person nor her dress were disordered?

A: Not that I saw.

Q: The deceased appeared very calm and in very good spirits?

A: Yes.

Mary changed her clothes in front of Hannah, pulling off her white stockings while standing and chatting, and tied everything up in a handkerchief along with her purchases from Birmingham market. She wrapped her boots in another handkerchief and kept her white shoes on. She said nothing to Hannah about starting her period.

Now it was the turn of the defence. Defence counsel were limited in their powers. They could only cross-examine on matters of fact and until 1898 the defendant could not give sworn evidence under oath. William Reader asked about what Mary had told Hannah about where she had been since they parted on the Chester Road:

Q: When the deceased came and called you up in the morning, where did she say she had been?

A: She told me she had slept at her grandfather's.

Q: Did you say anything to the deceased, when she had called you up, about the prisoner?

A: I asked her how long Mr Thornton stopped, and she said a good bit.

Q: Did you say anything else to her about the prisoner?

A: I asked her what had become of him.

Q: What answer did she make?

A: She said he was gone home.

In reality, Mary had neither spent the small hours with her grandfather nor stopped there on the way home to Langley Heath. She had lied. Reader's aim was to chip away at Mary's reputation for 'honesty'.

Apart from stating that he had seen Mary dancing with Thornton at the Tyburn, Benjamin Carter merely corroborated Hannah's story about walking down the Chester Road. It was the account given by the next witness, John Humpage, who was the last person to see Thornton and Mary together, that had most impact and also proved to be the most confusing. Humpage said that at around two o'clock, while he was inside the cottage next to Lavell's, he heard people talking outside in Penns Mill Lane. This was a variation on the story he gave at the inquest when he said he was on his way home and saw a woman's light-coloured dress through the hedge while he was in the Lane. Either way, his evidence suggested that early in the morning Mary and Thornton had been in the fields behind Penns Lane before he came across them at around 3.15 at the stile. As he passed, he was greeted by Thornton but Mary held her head down. Reynolds' first focus in cross-examination was the distance between the house Humpage had been visiting and the pit. Humpage said it was a hundred yards (it was actually more like two to three hundred). Without saying so, he was exploring the issue of rape. If Thornton had raped Mary at this time, why did she did not scream — Humpage would surely have heard her — or, if she was being maltreated by Thornton why she did not appeal to Humpage for help as he walked by?

Thereafter a series of witnesses described seeing Mary walking down towards Erdington or coming away from it. Thomas Asprey saw her at half-past three near Greensall's just south of the junction with Holly Lane as she walked speedily and alone in the direction of Mrs Butler's house.

> Q: (John Singleton Copley) Did you see any other person about there?
>
> A: No.
>
> Q: How wide is Bell Lane there?
>
> A: About twenty-one yards.
>
> Q: Is it straight?
>
> A: Yes, for a considerable distance.

If Thornton was lurking, he was not seen.

John Kesterton, a teamster for Thomas Greensall, had taken some horses up to the horsepit on Bell Lane, turned them round in the road and was coming back through Erdington when he saw Mary emerge from Mrs Butler's at 4.15. He cracked his whip to attract her attention and she looked up towards him. He noticed that she seemed to be in a hurry. The road was very broad at that point and, like Asprey, he saw no one else about. Joseph Dawson saw Mary a moment later, and asked her how she was. He noticed her straw bonnet and red spencer and the fact that she was walking very fast. She was alone. Thomas Broadhurst saw her a few minutes later at the junction of Bell Lane and the Chester Road and also noted that she was walking fast. After this George Jackson described finding Mary's bonnet, bundle and shoes by the pit, going to fetch William Lavell and afterwards coming across the blood. From the pit to the footpath he saw a zig-zag of blood, two yards in length, and the lake of blood by the side of a bush, with more to the left.

The evidence of William Lavell was the cornerstone of the prosecution case. His tracking and interpretation of the footmarks in the ploughed field would prove that Thornton had chased and subdued Mary, and the person-shaped impression in the dewy grass under the tree by the footpath would prove the attack. However, rather than letting this quiet, intelligent man describe his findings at length, Clarke fired short, closed questions at him, eliciting short, closed answers. Confusing to the reader now, they must have been almost bewildering to the jury in court.

Despite this, Lavell managed to tell the court that he had traced the footsteps of the man and woman dodging on and off the footpath just before it turned into the harrowed field, then running up the side towards the dry pit. After the man and woman turned right at the top of the field going towards the fatal pit, the impressions in the ground indicated that they were sometimes walking, sometimes dodging and sometimes running. After they passed the first marl pit on the left, the woman's footsteps were found no longer and she did not come back that way. From there to the stile Lavell could find only the man's footsteps. He discovered a second trail of footmarks, of the man only, going back across the top of the field towards the dry pit and then diverting across the field to the bottom right-hand corner, an exit leading to Pipe Hall and on towards the Chester Road. It was a shortcut across private land but from the Chester Road a person could easily reach the canal towpath and get down to Holden's farm.

Clarke asked about the comparison of Thornton's shoes to the footmarks. Lavell said he had compared a dozen impressions in three different locations. He had 'no doubt at all' that they were an exact match.

Q: Had those shoes, either of them, any particular nail?

A: There was a sparrow-nail.

Q: Was there any at the toe of either shoe?

A: There is not on one side.

Q: Which shoe?

A: The right.

Q: Were there any marks of this sparrow-nail on those [footmarks] that you covered [with the boards]?

A: There was one step trod on a short stick which throwed [sic] the foot up, and there were the marks of two nails.

He and Bird had also compared Mary's shoes, and found that they corresponded with the smaller footprints. For a reason he did not explain, or which was not recorded by the shorthand writers, he did not fit Thornton's shoe into the single footmark by the pit.

There was detailed questioning about the 'lake of blood' and the trail of blood leading to the pit, which Lavell described as running straight up towards the pit across the path and then about a foot from the path, on the clover. There were no footsteps near the blood. Was it a track or a few drops? asked Clarke. 'It came in drops at last, but it was a regular run where it first came on the clover,' replied Lavell.

Up to this point the defence's questioning had been routine, even desultory, as if the Reader and Reynolds were merely going through the motions. They had been holding fire for Lavell and Bird. Reader cross-examined, questioning Lavell about the distance from the pit to his house and about the rain that had fallen in the middle of the morning. In his brief for the barristers, Sadler wrote that before Thornton's and Mary's shoes were tested there had been a violent thunderstorm, 'the severest… we have had this summer', that only two footmarks were covered on the harrowed ground, neither of them the woman's. He suggested that many of the footmarks in the field were Lavell and Bird's own or were made by the crowds of villagers who had gathered in the field once the word got out.

Q: There were a great many people collected in the ploughed field, were there not?

A: At one time after another; but not then.

Q: Do you think there were more than one thousand footsteps then.

A: Not then.

Reader persisted.

> Q: Were there not a great many other footsteps beside the steps you had traced in the morning?
>
> A: Yes, there were a great many.
>
> Q: Some thousands perhaps.
>
> A: I won't say thousands.
>
> Q: Were there not a great number of footmarks of other persons?
>
> A: Yes.

Lavell was forced to admit that he did not try Thornton's shoes with the marks he supposed that other people had made. His seemingly careful analysis had failed to spot that, sparrow-nails apart, Thornton's shoes may have fitted into almost any other male footmark. Reader tried a series of tacks, flitting from one matter to another in a deliberate attempt to disconcert Lavell, first asking him about the blood, then the single footmark, then the footsteps across the harrowed field and the route to Castle Bromwich, then the blood again and finally the single footmark once more.

Joseph Bird was also examined on the footprints. His stolid and detailed replies to John Copley's questioning entirely corroborated Lavell's account. The man was on the right of the woman, he said, and in places they had been running.

> Q: What makes you think that the persons had been running?
>
> A: By the length of the stride, and by the little scrape at the toe of the woman's shoe. The heels of the man's shoe sunk very deep, as if made by a heavy man.

Bird described in detail how he had compared the man's footsteps with Thornton's shoe.

> 'I kneeled down and blew the dirt out of the right footstep to see if there were any nail marks. There lay a bit of rotten wood across the footstep, which had turned the outside of the shoe a little up, and the impression on that side of the foot was not so deep as the other. I observed two nail marks on that side where it was shallowest. The shoes were nailed and there was a space of about two inches where the nails were out, and they were

49

> nailed again…I marked the first nail on the side of the shoe, and
> then kneeled down to see if they exactly corresponded, and they
> did exactly. I could see the second nail mark at the same time,
> as well as under the shoe and they fitted every part exactly.'

He did the same with the woman's footmarks and Mary's white shoes.

> 'Where the running over the ground was, there was a dent
> or scraping in the ground, and by looking at the shoes, the
> leather of one shoe was raised at the toe more than the other,
> from being wet. The shoes were not alike, and the impressions
> varied accordingly, agreeing with the form of each shoe.'

Copley asked Bird about the route that seemed to have been taken by the man across the harrowed field. There is no regular footpath there, he said, and described how someone might get to the bridge across the Birmingham and Fazeley Canal south of Tyburn by following a road 'near Samuel Smith's house, which is used by market people.' Anybody might use it to reach Holden's farm.

Henry Reynolds cross-examined him. 'Men walk in many different ways, don't they,' he said. 'Some upright, some rather on their heels, some leaning forwards upon their toes, some take long steps and some short ones?' Bird agreed. 'And some take quite as long strides when they walk, as when they run?' continued Reynolds. 'I never saw a man take longer steps in walking than he did in running,' shot back Bird. Reynolds changed the subject, now addressing the thunderstorm that had fallen that morning. Bird said it had rained 'sharpish' but there had been no thunderstorm. What about the people in the field? How many were there? A hundred perhaps? 'No,' said Bird. Thirty or forty, and Mr Bedford, who had arrived between nine and ten o'clock, when there were only twenty people there, had ordered them to stay away from the footmarks.

After James Simmons described using a heel rake and reins to retrieve Mary's body and the state of the body ('There was a little mud and some old oak leaves on the face') it was the turn of Joseph Webster. He told the court that he came to the pit soon after he was alerted that a woman had drowned in it, witnessed the body being taken out of the water and ordered his men to take it to Lavell's cottage. By the tree he saw what he described as 'a considerable quantity of blood' which 'lay in a round space, and was as large as I could cover with my extended hand.' It was 'much coagulated'. He also saw the impression of a 'human figure on the grass' with arms and legs 'stretched out their full length' and a small quantity of blood at the centre. He saw the marks of the toes of a man's large shoes at the bottom of the figure and he traced the blood for ten yards up by the side of the path towards the pit. Joseph Bird showed him the footmarks in the harrowed field, after which he sent for Mary's shoes. One of the shoes was bloodstained on both inside and out. The shoes were produced and passed to the jury and then up to the Judge. The stain on the inside was clearly seen but that on the outside, as you might expect with leather shoes, had faded. Webster also described the 'marks from the grasp of a man's hand' he had seen on Mary's arms after the spencer was taken off and blood on the seat of the pink gown. 'It was in a very dirty state. There was blood also on other parts of the gown,' he said. Later he had gone to see Hannah Cox and measured the accuracy of her mother's clock which he found to be forty-one minutes fast.

Fanny Lavell was the first female to give evidence, a lone woman in an overwhelmingly male environment. She had to talk about matters that were generally only women's business, but she was a capable, down-to-earth person, and she did not hesitate. She told the court that she had undressed Mary's body and had had to tear off some of her clothes. 'The gown she had on was very dirty — blood and dirt,' she said, but she could not see blood on the black stockings. As at the inquest, Thomas Dales then produced the pink dress, and the court saw that the seat was stained with blood and dirt, just as Fanny had said. The white undershift was the same. The white party clothes were also produced. The dress had blood on the back of the skirt but the white spencer was clean. There were spots of blood on the white stockings.

Mary Smith, who had helped Fanny, was called next and mentioned the black marks on Mary's arms. When she examined the lower parts of the body, she said, she found it in 'a very bloody state' but could not tell whether it was from 'a monthly evacuation or blood from violence.' She thought that the body was not yet cold.

It was late afternoon by now. At some point Thornton requested refreshment and we can speculate that this was a convenient point to break, before Mr Bedford was questioned. There was no awkward cross-examination this time, no Sadler to needle him on inaccuracies or changes to the statement. He simply said that the Prisoner made a deposition, after which an officer of the court read it out (a version is given on page 132).

It was the performance of Thomas Dales, the assistant constable, who appeared next, that was to prove the most controversial of the whole trial.

He seemed to have suffered a lapse of memory about events after he took Thornton into custody at Tyburn House.

> Q: (John Singleton Copley) [Before Mr Bedford arrived] what did you say to him [Thornton]?
>
> A: I don't recollect — nothing in particular... I just don't remember. We were all talking together for some time. I told him he was my prisoner.
>
> Q: Nothing in particular — you say you had some conversation with him. What did you say to him?
>
> A: I just don't remember. We were all talking together for some time. I told him he was my prisoner.

He even seemed reluctant to identify those who came upstairs with him when he examined Thornton's clothing.

> Q: Who went — anybody but you and the prisoner?
>
> A: The Prisoner, myself and William Bedson.
>
> Q: Anybody else? Did nobody go up with you into the room?
>
> A: Yes, Mr Sadler went into the room with us.

He told the court that Thornton's breeches and shirt were both 'very much stained', and that he had offered an explanation: 'He said he had been concerned with the girl, by her own consent, but he knew nothing about the murder.' Later, when Copley pressed him again on what he and the prisoner had talked about in the hour or so before Mr Bedford arrived, he said again: 'Nothing in particular, I remember he said, when he was before Mr Bedford...' at which point he was cut off by Mr Reynolds for the defence, who objected that no oral addition to Thornton's written statement should be accepted. Dales's account of what was said during Thornton's interview with Mr Bedford was ruled irrelevant. The judge agreed, and after a discussion Judge Holroyd decided, for reasons that were not shared, that Thornton's clothes should not be put into evidence.

Now it was the turn of William Reader to cross-examine Dales on Thornton's admission of a 'connection' with Mary. Did Thornton confess to this *before* he was taken in front of Bedford to be examined? Dales seemed unsure.

One of several idealised portraits of Mary Ashford created after her death.

When the case reached London, interest in Abraham Thornton was so great that the *Observer* went to the expense of publishing a portrait of him.

Hannah Cox's mother Mrs Butler lived at Erdington Green in a dwelling similar in design to these surviving cottages in Station Road.

The Whitsuntide dance where Abraham Thornton and Mary Ashford met was held in the annex of Tyburn House on the Chester Road.

Thornton lived with his family at Shard End, a farm near Castle Bromwich.

An eighteenth-century view of Birmingham – industry was beginning to encroach on its suburban villages.

FIELDS ON AN ENLARGED SCALE

PEN'S MILL LANE

FATAL FIELD

HARROWED FIELD

Fatal Pit

Scale of yards

A SECTION OF THE PIT

Scale of feet

Situation of the body when found

Footpath

Castle Bromwich Church

Townleys Mill

Thorn house

to Castle Bromwich

Birmingham & Fazeley Canal

Farmhouse

Fisheries

LONDON & CHESTER ROAD

Supposed track of the Murderer

Pens Mill

to Lougley Mary's house

Lovells & Reynolds

Fatal Field

Harrowed Field

Grimleys

Moors Grandfathers

Freemans

PEN'S MILL LANE

BELL LANE

Bell & Cuckoo

to Lichfield

Bing Lane

Penky Lane

Greensville

Workhouse

Butchers

Swan Inn

Crackers

ERDINGTON

to Birmingham

Alum Pit

High Lane

Foot path

Foot path

Just Thornton says he took after leaving Way

The road

LICHFIELD & BIRMINGHAM ROAD

Scale of yards

Surveyed by Rowland Hill & George Morcroft Birmingham. & Published Nov. 21. 1817 as the Acts: for Hearthote & Foster. Warwick.

Map created in 1818 by Rowland Hill and George Morecroft showing key locations in the murder. The detail of footmarks in the harrowed field and the 'fatal field' reflect the investigations of William Lavell and Joseph Bird, two employees at the nearby wire drawing factory.

On the right-hand side of the map is Tyburn House where Mary Ashford encountered Abraham Thornton on 26 May 1817 at a Whitsuntide party. They left in the company of Hannah Cox and Benjamin Carter and walked together along the London and Chester Road as far as Old Cuckoo, where Hannah Cox left the others and followed the road leading to Erdington. Carter went on home, past the crossroads.

The next time Thornton and Mary Ashford were seen was about 3am, by John Humpage, at the stile marked A at the top of the foredrove leading into Bell Lane (left-hand side of the map, near to the top). The foredrove leads to a footpath which passes through the fields and then joins Penns Mill Lane, the road to Langley, where Mary lived with her uncle. Later as he crossed Bell Lane at Greensall's, Thomas Asprey saw Mary walking alone down Bell Lane.

After Mary reached Mrs Butler's at Erdington Green, she called up to Hannah Cox, and changed her clothes. A few minutes later Kesterton saw her come out of Mrs Butler's house and turn up Bell Lane. Dawson saw her and spoke to her between Mrs Butler's and Greensall's. Broadhurst saw her near where Bell Lane crosses the Chester Road; here she passed a second time by her grandfather's; and, it is supposed, turned down the foredrove and go through the fields, that being the shortest way home.

In his deposition, Thornton said that he walked with Mary from the stile marked A where they were seen by Humpage, down Bell Lane to Erdington Green, marked B, near to Mrs Butler's, where he waited for about five minutes and then went home by the road marked on the map, leading to Holden's.

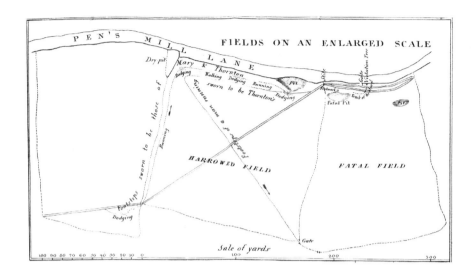

Detail of Hill's map showing marks in the field in which Mary died. The prosecution claimed that Thornton exited the harrowed field in the bottom right corner and crossed trespass land.

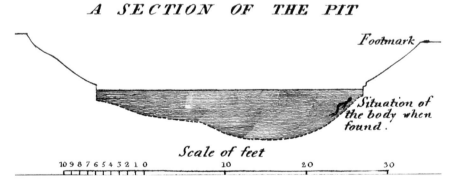

Rowland Hill's cross-section of the pit showing the position of the footmark and of Mary's body.

Illustration of the scene showing the footpath in the centre, the pit on the left and the 'violation tree' and a view through to Penns Mill Lane on the right.

The 'murder pit' photographed in 1902.

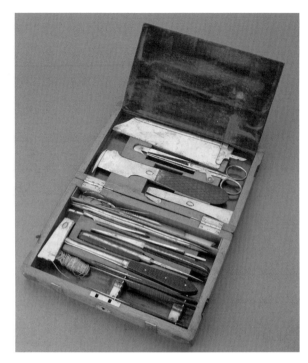

Left: Many surgeons owned portable autopsy kits – this one was made in 1860.

Below: Mary's gravestone at Sutton Coldfield Church was inscribed with a moralistic admonition written by the Reverend Luke Booker.

Above: New Street, Birmingham, where solicitors William Bedford and his nephew John had offices.

Right: The Reverend Luke Booker defended Mary's name but felt that she was naïve and too independent.

Warwick Shire Hall on Northgate Street, where vast crowds of men gathered on 8 August 1817 hoping to see the trial of Abraham Thornton.

Westminster Hall, where Abraham Thornton appeared in answer William Ashford's appeal of murder at the Court of King's Bench.

ABRAHAM THORNTON.

Engraved by W. T. Fry.

While most portraits of Abraham Thornton showed him as brutish and unappealing, William Thomas Fry's was more sympathetic.

Above: A libertine master violently 'importunes' his virtuous maidservant.

Left: The case against Thornton took place against a backdrop of political strife and social upheaval. Jeremiah Brandreth suffered a traitor's death for his protests.

Right: After her death Mary was presented to the middle-classes as an icon of female working-class virtue and her image was accordingly idealised.

Below: A prison hulk at Plymouth, similar to the vessel Omar Hall was incarcerated in while he awaited transportation to New South Wales.

Above: Abraham Thornton threw down the fellow of this white leather fingerless gauntlet in answer to William Ashford's appeal of murder.

Right: A 1917 depiction of medieval trial by combat – Thornton and Ashford would have had to use cudgels.

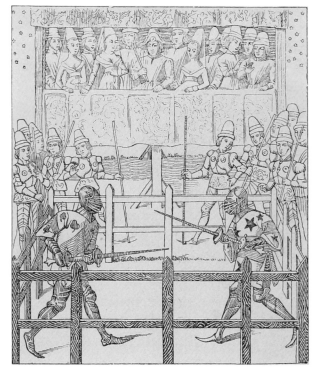

Right: Walter Scott incorporated trial by combat into the plot of his 1820 novel Ivanhoe.

Below: The public were used to hearing tales of illegal duelling between gentlemen but trial by combat was seen as a return to an uncouth medieval past.

Above: One of the many stage representations based on the case was *Trial by Battle; or, Heaven Defend the Right*, which was the opening performance of the Royal Coburg Theatre (bottom) in Lambeth Marsh on 11 May 1818.

A: Yes, he did. I believe he did.

Q: Did anyone hear it, besides yourself?

A: I can hardly tell. I think not. I don't recollect that anybody was present at that time.

Q: Did you tell Mr Bedford what the Prisoner had said, before he examined him?

A: No, I believe not.

In the courtroom, William Bedford must have been both dismayed and angry. To his mind, the assistant constable, about whom he already had doubts, had jeopardised the whole case. There was more confusion when Copley re-examined Dales.

Q: Did the Prisoner tell you that he had connection with the deceased before the magistrate came to Clarke's [Tyburn House]?

A: I'm not quite sure whether he said so before or after.

Q: You are sure he did say so to you, are you?

A: I'm sure he said so, when we were searching him upstairs.

Q: You are quite sure of that?

A: Yes.

Q: Who heard him make that confession besides yourself?

A: Mr Sadler and William Bedson were present.

Before the trial, while they were drinking in a pub, Joseph Cotterill had told Mary Ashford's father Thomas that Thornton had had his eye on her the minute she arrived at the dance. Cotterill himself either refused to appear as a witness or made himself so hard to find that a subpoena could not be served. It was a serious loss as his evidence would have established a motive for Thornton's attack. Bedford had managed to get the next best thing: John Cooke, a young Erdington farmer who had been at Tyburn House and overheard the conversation between Thornton and Cotterill. Clarke tried to make sure that that his story was credible.

Q: You were near enough to them [Cotterill and Thornton] to hear distinctly what was said?

A: Yes, I stood close to them.

> Q: Did anyone else hear the prisoner speak those words to Cotterill?
>
> A: No, I don't think they did.
>
> Q: But you stood near enough to them both, to hear what was said distinctly?
>
> A: Yes.

Reynolds, for the defence, responded with sarcasm, seeking to destroy Cooke as a reliable and respectable witness: 'Of course, you remonstrated with Thornton, on his making use of this expression, didn't you... Then you went immediately and told Mary Ashford what you had heard.' Thornton's alleged words were a 'dreadful threat', said Reynolds, assuming, or at least pretending to, that Cooke was bound by the social rules of Reynolds's own middle-class life. It is more likely that Cooke, who knew the Ashfords as neighbours, would merely have shrugged off this conversation, assuming that Mary could and would make up her own mind about Thornton and his intentions.

Daniel Clarke, the keeper of Tyburn House, told the court that after Twamley turned up at the inn enquiring about who Mary had left the previous night's party with, he had offered to go and find Thornton and came across him a mile down the road near the chapel in Castle Bromwich, riding a pony. Copley asked him what he had said to Thornton.

> A: I said to him, what is become of the young woman that went away with you from my house last night?
>
> Q: What reply did he make?
>
> A: He made no answer.
>
> Q: What did you say then?
>
> A: I said, she has been murdered and thrown into a pit.
>
> Q: Did the prisoner make any reply to that?
>
> A: He said 'Murdered!'. I said, 'Yes, murdered.'
>
> Q: What answer did the Prisoner make?
>
> A: The Prisoner said, 'I was with her till four o'clock this morning.'

Clarke told him that he must come to Tyburn to clear himself and Thornton replied that he could 'soon do that' so they rode towards the inn.

Q: What then did you talk about?

A: Things as we saw, as we passed along.

Q: What things?

A: We talked about farming.

Reader asked Clarke to speculate on whether Thornton had already known about Mary's death. 'No, I don't think he had,' said Clarke. Thornton had volunteered the information that he had been with Mary 'without any consideration'? Yes indeed. Judge Holroyd jumped in here and asked whether Thornton had appeared confused at the news. 'Yes I think he appeared a little confused.' 'Persons in general, labouring under any very great distress of mind, are not inclined to talk much, are they?' suggested Reader and Clarke agreed.

Daniel Clarke's evidence was perfect for the defence. He had painted a picture of Thornton as a sober, thoughtful and truthful young man, who had voluntarily given information about Mary. Most members of the court would be of the opinion that Thornton's behaviour to Mary was to be regretted, but it was perfectly understandable, given that the girl was willing. He was a normal young man with normal urges. Who among them would not have done the same?

More items were shown in evidence. William Lavell was recalled to identify Mary's half-boots which were found in the bundle by the pit, and the black stockings she was wearing when she was pulled out of the water. These were handed around to the judge and jury, as were Thornton's shoes. The judge said the stockings seemed perfectly clean except for one or two spots which he thought he could just perceive on one of them. The courtroom must have been perplexed, but rapidly coming to a conclusion. If the white stockings were bloodstained and the black stockings were not, how could this be reconciled with the prosecution's case? The blood on the white ones must be hymen blood, proving that the sex with Thornton was consensual. On the other hand, if she had sex while wearing the white frock why was it less bloody than the pink one, which she was wearing when she was pulled out of the pit? Perhaps that blood was menstrual and nothing to do with the sexual intercourse.

The prosecution case was drawing to a close. The final witness, the surgeon George Freer, described going with his colleague Richard Horton to see Mary's body at the Lavells' cottage, asking for it to be moved to a better location, and then visiting the scene, where he saw 'a quantity of blood lying in various places near the pit'. When the surgeons returned on Thursday to perform the post-mortem, the upper surface of Mary's body had been washed but between the thighs and the lower parts of the legs, there was a great deal of blood. He told the court that there were lacerations on the vagina as well as coagulated blood. He opened the body and confirmed that Mary had been menstruating, and from the fluid in her stomach concluded that the cause of death was drowning. In his opinion, the blood in the field was from the lacerations but those injuries were not serious enough to cause her death. As for Mary's monthly flow it had probably been brought on earlier than she had expected (hence the lack of cloth) and it had not resulted from sexual intercourse.

There was a marked contrast in the way Clarke asked questions of Freer to his questioning of Lavell, Bird, Nathaniel Gooding and the other working-class witnesses. 'Be good enough to describe to us the state in which you found the body,' he said, and later, 'In your judgment, what was the cause of the deceased's death?' Freer spoke expansively each time, explaining his findings without interruption.

The defence team did not cross-examine Freer and here the prosecution case closed. Before the defence began, two maps were presented, one prepared for the prosecution by the Erdington surveyor William Fowler and the other, for the defence, by Henry Jacobs of Birmingham, who said he had measured the distances with a chain and was satisfied that they were perfectly correct.

Chapter 7

Defence

Thornton's defence rested entirely on his alibi. If he was not in the harrowed field when Mary came through it on her way to her uncle's, he could not have murdered her. In his brief for Thornton's barristers Sadler had laid it out clearly: 'The only point the Prisoner can in this case rest his defence on is the improbability and even impossibility of his committing the offence on account of the very short period of time that did elapse after the deceased left Butler's house in the morning and before he was seen near John Holden's house.' Even if Mary left Mrs Butler's house as early as four o'clock and reached the pit fifteen or twenty minutes later, Thornton would only have about fifteen minutes to rape and murder her, arrange her belongings on the bank and get to Holden's farm three and a half miles away.

Even so, it was crucial for the defence to establish that Thornton was seen at Holden's farm as early as they could and that he had not been running. William Jennens, the Birmingham milkman, confirmed that he had seen Thornton at 'about half past four o'clock, as near as I could judge, having no watch.' How did you know what time it was? asked Reader.

> A: My wife, who was with me, afterwards asked at Mr Holden, of Jane Heaton, the servant, what o'clock it was. She looked at the clock and told her.
>
> Q: How long was it, after you saw the Prisoner, before your wife asked Jane Heaton what time it was?
>
> A: Before she inquired, and after I saw the Prisoner, we had milked a cow a piece, in the yard, which might occupy us about ten minutes. The cows were not in the yard then, they were a field's breadth from the house.
>
> Q: And you think this time, in all, took up about ten minutes.
>
> A: Yes, about ten minutes altogether.

Jennens said Thornton was walking 'very leisurely… quite slow' but Clarke, for the prosecution, was more interested in which direction he came from: the towing path of the canal or down the lane. 'I can't tell that. I did not see him until he was within twenty yards of me,' said William Jennens but immediately contradicted himself when Reader asked how far down the towpath he could see ('Three or four hundred yards') and whether Thornton had come that way ('I think I must [would] have seen him').

Martha Jennens also said she had seen Thornton, who was 'coming along gently' and corroborated her husband's account of milking the cows and asking Jane Heaton the time. But to Copley, cross-examining for the prosecution, she admitted that she had had her back to Thornton initially, while she and her husband 'looked at a cow that was running at a great rate down the lane' and only saw Thornton when they turned round to look after the animal. She agreed that he could have come along the towpath.

John Holden's servant Jane Heaton said she rose at 4.30 and as she stood at a window in the farmhouse saw a man walking 'quite slow' along the road leading from Erdington to Castle Bromwich. She remembered Martha Jennens asking her the time, and said she told her it was seventeen minutes to five. John Holden junior told the court he had gone to fetch the cows for the Jennens to milk 'but I don't know what time they came.' He claimed to know Thornton by sight and said he saw him two hundred yards from the farmhouse going 'quite slow' towards Castle Bromwich.

William Twamley, now totally estranged from William Bedford, spoke about checking John Holden's clock, which matched his own exactly. 'I went from thence to Birmingham. My watch was just right with St Martin's church, and it wanted a minute and a half of the tower clock there.'

The next sighting of Thornton was by the floodgates at Zachariah Twamley's mill, half a mile from Holden's farm, when he stopped to talk to his friend John Heydon, who was Mr Rotton's gamekeeper. Heydon told the court he had left his home at ten to five and went to empty the nets he had put down the night before. He heard Rotton's stable clock strike five and saw Thornton coming along the footpath towards Castle Bromwich five minutes after that. Heydon asked him where he had been. 'Taking a wench home,' he replied (according to his own statement, Thornton had not actually done that; he claimed he had parted with Mary near Greensall's farm while he relieved himself in a field, and did not see her again). John Woodcock, Zachariah Twamley's miller, said he saw Thornton and Heydon talking. 'From a calculation I have since made, it must have been about ten minutes past five.' When questioned by Copley for the prosecution, he explained, 'I went into the mill the first thing, and when I came out again, I heard Mr Rotton's stable clock strike five. I then went into a piece of wheat belonging to Mr Smallwood, and came back again. It must have been soon after five when I saw the Prisoner come up to Heydon at the floodgates, for I have walked the ground over since, and it takes me just ten minutes at a gentle pace.'

Joseph Webster's brother-in-law John William Crompton told the court that he had measured the clock at Castle Bromwich church and found it to be a quarter of an hour fast; James White, at work at Wheelwright's bank, half a mile from Twamley's mill, saw Thornton at 5.20 going towards Castle Bromwich. Finally, William Coleman, Mary's grandfather, truthfully stated that Mary had not slept at his house on the night of 26 May. Calling him was an act of cruelty on the part of the defence. It added nothing to Thornton's defence, but established the victim as a liar.

It was six o'clock. All that remained now was for the judge to deliver the charge to the jury and to sum up the evidence.

Justice Holroyd started with worthy exhortations not to convict on anything but the facts and to ignore any prejudice. It was not a question of whether the prisoner had moral responsibility for Mary's death, he said, but whether he had actually murdered her. He acknowledged that many prosecutions were built on evidence that was entirely circumstantial, as this one was, but at the same time, 'facts could not be altered; they always spoke for themselves, and would not give way to opinions. But these circumstances... must be clear, full and perfect.'

The issue of whether the sex took place before or after Mary went to Mrs Butler's to change her clothes was key. If the jury thought it took place before, the sex was consensual because Mary showed no distress when she was with Hannah. They should remember that if that was the case, Thornton would have had no motive to kill her. 'If there was no rape, and the intercourse took place with the consent of the deceased, whether that consent was obtained by great importunity or not, that would make it less likely that [Thornton] would commit murder,' he said. Importunity was not regarded as violence, but was a step up from seduction or emotional pressure and arose from Thornton's need to complete a sexual act that Mary, by cavorting in fields, had semi-promised. Holroyd had encapsulated the essence of rape law. It was, after all, almost impossible to rape a woman. Any coercion to overcome Mary's understandable reluctance fell within the bounds of legality.

If the sex took place after Mary had changed her clothes, Holroyd conceded only that it was more likely to be rape. But in any case, if

Thornton's witnesses were telling the truth, he was several miles away when Mary went into the pit. This made 'what space of time there was for the transactions to take place…very material.'

Holroyd used the plan of the area (we don't know whether it was the defence or the prosecution's version) to point out places and distances. In the end, however, it boiled it down to this: 'It is your duty to consider whether it is possible for the pursuit [of Mary in the harrowed field] to have taken place, and all the circumstances connected with it, and for the prisoner to have reached Holden's house, a distance of nearly three miles and a half, in so short a time — a period of not more than twenty minutes.' It was better, he said in conclusion, that the murderer, 'with all the weight of his crime upon his head, should escape punishment, than that another person should suffer death, without being guilty.' As for the alibi, it must be 'clear, certain and well connected, there must be no blank in the chain, or else all would fall to the ground.'

At 8.30pm, twelve and a half hours after the process started, the jury left the courtroom, returning six minutes later to announce a verdict of Not Guilty. For the first time since he had entered the courtroom Thornton betrayed some emotion. The relief showed on his face.

The rest of the trial was a formality. Thornton was charged with rape and, after the prosecution offered no evidence, was again acquitted. He left the court a free man.

PART 2

Chapter 8

Evidence

'The acquittal of Thornton, in this atrocious rape and murder, has excited the most undisguised feelings of disappointment in all classes of people, from one end of the country to the other,' reported the *Lichfield Mercury*, whose forthright editor James Amphlett was taking a keen interest in the case. Over at the vicarage in Dudley, a town ten miles (16km) to the north-west of Birmingham, the Reverend Luke Booker and his parishioners were lamenting the verdict. It was the only subject of conversation in every cottage and every drawing room, and even, Booker added, 'among companies consisting of both sexes'. He himself was so disgusted that he felt compelled to make things right by raising money for a suitable gravestone for Mary's final resting place.

It was as if the trial, and the injustice of its result, spoke directly to a fractured and anxious country in need of a common cause; antipathy towards Thornton was an emotional umbrella under which everyone, from the top of society to the bottom, could unite in righteous opposition. Sometimes, however, popular defence of a female could go too far and alarm the authorities. In 1814 the body of another young woman, twenty-year-old Lavinia Robinson, was found on the banks of the River Irwel seven weeks after she went missing from her home in Manchester. Like Mary, Lavinia was praised for her beauty and personality, but unlike with Mary there was no real suspicion that she had been murdered. The assault had been on her reputation. Lavinia's fiancé, who worked as an accoucheur (man-midwife) at Manchester's Lying-In Hospital, and was named, ironically enough, John Holroyd, had accused her of a 'lack of chastity' with a previous admirer. Shamed and mortified, she left her siblings a note ('With my last dying breath, I attest myself innocent of the crime laid to my charge. God bless you all, I cannot outlive his suspicion.') and threw herself in the water. The Manchester newspapers commiserated with Lavinia's family while she was missing and eulogised her after her death, but it was the mob, frighteningly, who took action. After the inquest, they scrawled graffiti on the doors and walls of Holroyd's lodgings and threw stones at the windows. 'A kind of fury seemed to hang on the minds of the lower classes of society, which threatened most serious consequences to Mr Holroyd,' reported *Bell's Weekly Messenger.* Holroyd was sacked by the trustees of the hospital and, fearful for his safety, sought protection at the police office and later, on their advice, left the city.

Lavinia's fiancé had been untouchable. All that could be done was to hound the scoundrel out of his job and home. For Mary's self-appointed champion, William Bedford, smarting from Thornton's escape from justice, the story was not over. After the trial Thornton was free to resume his former life. William Bedford took this as a personal defeat. Already suspicious of Thomas Dales after his behaviour at Tyburn House, Bedford decided who was to blame for Thornton's acquittal; the Birmingham thieftaker, whose testimony at the trial had been weak, incompetent and possibly corrupt. Within days of the trial, Bedford had arranged a meeting of his fellow magistrates at the Birmingham police office in Moor Street for 'a minute investigation of the facts', at the end of which they judged Dales guilty of gross misconduct and dismissed him from the police office with great disgrace.

Only now could Bedford begin to explore what was to be done about Thornton. Although most people assumed a defendant could not be put in double jeopardy, that is, he could not be tried twice for the same crime there was an arcane process that might provide redress. In mid-August *The Independent Whig*, while careful to absolve the judge and jury at Warwick of bias, declared that the Thornton trial had excited 'our sympathy, our horror, and our surprise' and hinted that 'in cases of murder, the next of kin can demand a second trial, provided they are dissatisfied with the verdict of acquittal.'

Appeal of murder (or appeal of death), the process alluded to by *The Independent Whig*, allowed an 'heir-at-law' of the victim (generally the closest male relative or in some cases a wife) to lodge an appeal, within a year and a day of the felony trial. The defendant, or appellee as he was known, was not disqualified by being previously acquitted so there was nothing to prevent him facing the same charge again. An appeal of murder was not a review of the original verdict; rather, the word appeal was derived from the French verb *appeller*, meaning to call out; it signified a challenge or summons. Essentially it was an opportunity for families to express an accusation for a heinous and unsatisfied crime in order to punish the offender for injury done to them. Crucially, it was not a Crown prosecution but a civil process, a hangover from legislation from the reigns of Edward III and Henry VII, over which the king had no control and for which he could not issue pardons. If Thornton was found guilty at a second trial, he would hang. He could not be reprieved.

Appeals of murder were rare, but there had been a few within living memory. On Christmas Eve 1769 two young Irishmen, Patrick and Matthew Kennedy, had indulged in some horseplay during which they fractured the skull of Mr Bigby, a watchman on Westminster Bridge, with a poker they had stolen from a public house. The brothers were tried for murder and would have hanged if it had not been for the influence of their sister Kitty, a courtesan under the protection of Lord Robert Spencer. The Kennedys were sentenced to transportation for life but Kitty wanted a royal pardon for them and persuaded her lover to induce his brother, the Duke of Marlborough, to ask the king for one. In opposition, the Bill of Rights Society financed a writ of appeal on behalf of Bigby's widow. Kitty once again came to the rescue and bribed the widow not to appear, which led to the collapse of the case. The Kennedy brothers were not, in the event, transported but were persuaded to take commissions in foreign armies.

Fifty years earlier, James Cluff (or Clough) was made to undergo a second trial after he was acquitted of murder in 1729. While employed at a public house in Holborn he began a relationship with Mary Green. He soon became abusive and regularly beat her. On 11 April, she was stabbed at the pub. The wound to her thigh, made through her clothes (an apron, a quilted coat and a thick petticoat), was five inches deep. Cluff's defence was that when he and Mary were in the cellar there had been a minor contretemps after which he went outside. On his return, he found Mary in one of the booths with her head on the table. She said, 'I am a dead woman' before collapsing. His story, from which he could not be moved, was that he had seen her with a knife in the cellar and that she must have stabbed herself. Several witnesses proved that Cluff had not seemed bad tempered that day, despite the arrival at the pub in the morning of a man who claimed to be Mary's sweetheart and who sat at the bar canoodling with her within his view. After Cluff was acquitted, Mary's brother William launched an appeal. Cluff was once again tried at the Old Bailey and this time found guilty and sentenced to death. In Newgate Prison, he refused to admit guilt or show remorse. He was hanged at Tyburn.

By the middle of August, Bedford had decided on a course of action, supported by a collection of independent gentlemen of the neighbourhood including Joseph Webster, Luke Booker of Dudley, as well as, in London, Sir Matthew Wood, the owner and editor of *The Independent Whig*. On 25 August, *The Times* announced that 'the oppressive cloud on the unappeased sense of public justice' would soon be lifted.

In late September James Amphlett published a crude map of the area in the *Lichfield Mercury* using glyphs and symbols of type rather than a woodblock or copperplate. The paper also made the point that country clocks are proverbial for nothing but their variance from true time and from each other. 'Every farmer, in point of fact, has a measurement of time of his own, by which his movements and those of his family are regulated. Guided by this, he cares but little whether his clock and the sun are in unison.'

William Bedford gave his nephew John Yeend Bedford the task of preparing for and managing the appeal of murder. The project was immense and during the seven months of the process John Bedford did little other work, his days filled in chasing down the prosecution papers, obtaining opinions from experts in the narrow field of appeal of murder, drawing up briefs, tracking down and interviewing new witnesses, and meeting and corresponding with his uncle and other interested parties.

Mary's bereaved family were also an obligation, not just because they deserved compassion but because nothing could proceed legally without them. The Ashfords were uneducated, unsophisticated people and needed information, and reassurance, about what the next few months would bring. The prospect of dealing with legal papers, of travelling to London, of appearing in court must have been daunting, especially as they were still recovering from the trauma of Mary's death and the disappointment of the verdict. Two weeks after the trial, John Bedford visited Mary's father Thomas to discuss the decision to start an appeal of murder and he saw him again five days later. On 9 September he travelled to Hints in Staffordshire, to see Mary's 23-year-old brother William, who had been identified as the appropriate heir-at-law. He was a poor, illiterate agricultural labourer, so a fund to cover legal costs was started, to which William Bedford fully expected to be the greatest contributor.

There were strong rumours in the neighbourhood that Thornton was preparing to emigrate, so the Bedfords had to move fast or they would be thwarted once more. John Bedford hurriedly wrote to the barrister and legal expert Sir Francis Const, Chairman of Westminster Sessions, to ask for guidance on the legal steps available to arrest Thornton. Const advised that since Judge Holroyd had discharged Thornton with no restrictions he could not simply be rearrested. Bedford would have to obtain a writ of appeal. Const also cautioned that the jury had been quick to acquit — the evidence had clearly not been enough to convict — and he was not convinced that a second trial would succeed. The Bedfords, or more likely William Bedford himself, took the decision to ignore his advice and plough on.

For a new trial to stand any chance, the Bedfords needed additional evidence. When it was clear that a second trial was a possibility, Thornton's former friends and neighbours, perhaps anxious at the prospect of living near a murderer, began to come forward with more information about him. On 8 September James Hope, a 29-year-old carpenter, wrote John Bedford a carefully penned note in which he related how he had been mowing a field of barley with five others including Abraham Thornton. He had had to take Thornton to one side and ask him to leave because 'everyone set their faces against him for he was sure to be taken up [arrested] again.' Thornton seemed to take it well. He calmly finished his swathe, laid down his scythe and put on his jacket. Hope told him that he knew of a place where he could lie low for a bit, but Thornton turned him down politely, instead asking Hope if he would like to dine with him that evening. Hope refused, perhaps because it was becoming apparent that friendship with Thornton could damage a man's reputation.

A few days later, Thornton sought Hope out at the end of the working day and while the two of them walked together towards Castle Bromwich Thornton told Hope that he did not murder Mary – 'she had fainted in his arms' – and that Sadler had advised him not to confess as he would be found guilty and hang. Thornton's account amounted to an admission that he had been with Mary after she left Mrs Butler's.

Having rejected Sir Francis Const's cautious approach, William Bedford talked through the plans for the writ of appeal with Nathaniel Gooding Clarke and sent his nephew John Bedford to London to see Joseph Chitty, a legal scholar he thought would be more favourable. This proved to be so, to some degree. The success of a second trial, wrote Chitty, would depend on the representations of the first trial judge and he advised Bedford, his fellow magistrates and their gentleman supporters to write to Holroyd setting out their feelings on the reinvestigation of the case. Whether they did this is unknown and it is entirely possible that they took the view that, given Holroyd's bias towards Thornton at Warwick, he was unlikely to help them. After all, the writ of appeal was, in effect, a criticism of Holroyd's conduct of the trial. What we do know is that John Bedford instructed his London agents to obtain a writ of appeal and started corresponding with the Under-Sheriff of Warwickshire about the guarantees into which William Ashford would have to enter. These were bonds between Ashford and his uncles John Coleman of Langley Heath and Charles Coleman of Erdington, who undertook to pay the Sheriff £100 if William failed to appear to prosecute his suit.

On 8 October, exactly two months after the Warwick trial, John Bedford received the writ of appeal and personally delivered it to the Under-Sheriff, who then issued a warrant for Abraham Thornton's arrest. Bedford took the warrant to Birmingham and gave it to John Hackney, the sheriff's officer, instructing him to execute it immediately.

At seven o'clock the following evening Hackney and two of his officers, Thomas Martin and Jonathan Baker, set out on the hour-long journey to Shard End. After stopping at a public house in Castle Bromwich, where they asked directions and enlisted a local man to come with them (without telling him their purpose), they arrived at the Thorntons' farmhouse. Martin and Baker stood guard outside while Hackney knocked and was let in by the family servant. When he asked for Mr Thornton she thought he meant Old Mr Thornton, and she told him that he had gone to bed but her mistress was in the kitchen. There Hackney found Mrs Thornton with her son and a friend.

'How do you do, Mr Thornton.'

'I am supposing that you wish to talk to my father,' he replied.

'No, I should be glad to speak to you,' said Hackney and at his request they moved off to the parlour, where he told him he had a warrant for his arrest and that he must come with him. Thornton was caught off-guard. Earlier that week, he said, he had been visited by two gentlemen (he did not name them) who told him that he should leave Castle Bromwich as soon as he could. He had refused. He confessed that he had not realised that all this would happen so quickly. His father was seriously ill and this may have affected his decision to delay his departure.

When the men returned to the kitchen, Mrs Thornton realised what was going on and threw up her hands, saying, 'That cruel Mr Bedford! What does he want with him? Isn't he satisfied now? We must thank him for all this.' It must have been a terrible scene. By now Martin and Baker had come in to the house to support Hackney while Thornton was being handcuffed. The prisoner was loudly complaining that the Bedfords and the Ashfords would only be satisfied when they had taken his life. He tried to calm his mother, telling her to 'make herself easy,' after which John Hackney and his officers took him away.

During the journey to Birmingham, where Thornton was to be held in custody at Hackney's own home in Bell Street which doubled as a lock-up, Hackney and Thornton talked about the case. Although he denied killing Mary, Thornton said several times that he 'believed if he had not gone with her it would not have happened' and repeated that 'she was as willing as he was.'

At about ten the next morning, Hackney and Martin took him in a chaise back to Warwick Gaol. When Hackney remarked that it was a pity he had not left for America as soon as the trial was over, Thornton replied that if he had known then as much as he did now, he certainly would have emigrated.

Much new information about Thornton came via James Amphlett of the *Lichfield Mercury*. On 18 October, he wrote to William Bedford about the 'great mass' of correspondence he had received from witnesses. He had been told that Zachariah Twamley's waggoner was prepared to swear that Thornton was not seen at the Mill until half past five, that another waggoner working for Mr Barton could contradict James White's evidence and that Daniel Clarke, the innkeeper at Tyburn House, did not disclose all of his conversation when he apprehended Thornton on the morning of the 27 May.

The quantity of new information may have been encouraging but its quality was disappointing. John Bedford was stopped in the street in Birmingham by William Burrish, a solicitor, who told him that Mr Shakespear, a glassmaker, had told him 'that he had been told by Mr Matthew Dixon, a plater from Snow Hill, who was one of the overseers of the poor of Birmingham, that Thornton had said to him (Mr Dixon) and some of the Birmingham overseers who were present at the time, that "He was with Mary Ashford after she changed her clothes."' Such vague, trivial hearsay or drunk-talk batted around in pubs, all needed investigating, requiring John Bedford or his clerk George Yates to go off on time-consuming expensive journeys, which usually turned out to be worthless, unusable in a court of law.

The Bedfords knew that for a second trial to succeed they needed proof either that the timings given by the defence were wrong or that Thornton's witnesses had lied. Any one of these leads might bring a breakthrough, so they must all be followed up. At times, it must have felt like trying to catch a will-o'-the-wisp.

John Bedford focused on the sighting of Thornton at Holden's farm as this was the first time Thornton was seen by a witness after John Humpage came across him with Mary at the stile in the foredrove. Did this really occur as early as William and Martha Jennens said it did and did it occur in the way they said it did?

At the Warwick trial, Young Holden stated that he saw Thornton two hundred yards from the farmhouse. In late August Peter Cheney, a Birmingham casting pot maker, was in the Rose and Crown in Moor Street with a group of men including John Holden senior, who told them, 'Thornton says he saw the milkman [William Jennens], and he saw my son, but my son did not see him.' Did Holden junior lie to the court? A few weeks later, again in the Rose and Crown, Robert Skynner, asked him about this. Holden senior flatly denied saying it. Then Cheney arrived and Skynner asked him whether he would back him up, at which Holden went silent, drank his ale and left. Perhaps now that Thornton had been arrested again, he felt that to protect his son from a possible charge of perjury he should keep his mouth shut.

Cheney's story was supported by John Stanley, an Erdington blacksmith, who said that a few days after the murder Holden junior told him he had not seen Thornton at all that morning. In fact, there was a question over whether Young Holden was even out of bed when Thornton passed the farm. Bedford made a note in the file: 'There is said to be a gent who heard Young Holden declare at market that he was in bed on the morning of the murder at six o'clock,' but what came of his inquiries is not known. However, Cheney soon afterwards arranged to see John Bedford to give a statement.

John Bedford also started looking in detail at the evidence given by William and Martha Jennens, the milk people who told the court they had seen Thornton 'walking very leisurely' and that 'he did not seem in a hurry, or the least confused.' William Sabin, a stirrup maker, said he had been drinking in the Wheatsheaf in Birmingham when the conversation turned to Thornton's trial and that one man, who said his name was Jennens, told him that he had been called to appear as a witness and pulled the subpoena out of his pocket to show him. He told Sabin that he and his wife Martha were going along the lane near Holden's farm when they heard the caw of magpies. Martha said it was a bad omen. Shortly afterwards they saw a cow running very fast and when they turned round to look at it they saw a man coming in great haste over the hedge of a field. Martha remarked on his appearance ('Look at that man's thick legs'). In early July Jennens repeated this story to William Edwards, who occasionally employed him in his garden in Birmingham. Jennens had told him that Thornton had 'passed them at a quick pace' and Martha had said, 'What a large pair of thick legs that man has got and that she did not like the look of him.' After the trial, when Edwards asked Jennens why he had not said anything about this, he merely offered, 'My wife would not let me say that.' There were also rumours that Jennens was not even at Holden's when Thornton passed. A certain Mr Vaughton said that Samuel Vale, a highly respectable Coventry alderman, was telling people that he could prove that Jennens had not left Birmingham on the morning of the murder, but he had no further details and the trail went cold.

John Woodcock, Zachariah Twamley's miller, had told the court at Warwick that he had calculated that it was 5.10am when he saw Thornton at the floodgates talking to John Heydon, Mr Rotton's gamekeeper. But there was another witness that morning: William Lawrence, Mr Twamley's waggoner, whose story had come to the attention of James Amphlett. When John Bedford spoke to him he declared that he was prepared to swear that he saw Thornton at 5.30. When asked why he was not asked to appear at Warwick, he said: 'My time would not suit them [Thornton and Sadler],' and that, 'If it had been me, I should have been hanged.'

There was also John Heels, a labourer from Erdington, who told James Hurber, a servant to Mr Laugher at Minworth, a village three and a half miles from Erdington, who told William Eggington that he saw Thornton walking up from Twamley's mill 'at a great pace', and that he had followed him for about two hundred yards as far as Mr Barton's gate, and at that time the Castle Bromwich clock struck six. He had known Thornton from birth so he had no doubts that it was him. He had not said anything about this earlier because 'the Thorntons always behaved well to me.'

69

Each one of these snippets of information bolstered the Bedfords' resolve in pursuing the case — they were grist to the mill. There were now also growing doubts about John Heydon, Mr Rotton's gamekeeper, who was a friend of Thornton's. In his evidence, Heydon had said that the Castle Bromwich clock struck five o'clock about five minutes before he saw Thornton. Elizabeth Ray, one of Rotton's maidservants (who was also the sister-in-law of Joseph Bird, who had investigated the footmarks in the field with William Lavell), told Joseph Webster that because it was wash day Heydon had lent them his watch so that they could get up early. He had asked them to rouse him early too, and this they did, at 4.45am. She said he could not possibly have left the house before five o'clock.

Among the most serious allegations, which were also the most difficult to verify, were claims about payments made by Abraham Thornton senior to jury members. Elizabeth Roberts, who worked in a Birmingham alehouse, wrote to William Bedford with her suspicions about four men who had sat on the jury: Thomas Johns, Isaac Green and Joseph Burge, all farmers in Lapworth, and George Tandy, from Hampton-in-Arden. They were 'not all that they should be,' she wrote, complaining that some of them also had family or friendship connections to the Thorntons.

An anonymous source told John Bedford that 'Mr Dowler of Castle Bromwich' had told him that after his acquittal, while drinking in a pub, Thornton had read out the trial report and stated how much each bit of the defence had cost him.

John Davis, the stonemason and friend of the Thornton family who had visited Abraham several times in Birmingham Gaol before he was taken off to Warwick, told a different version. He said that Thornton told him 'that the girl died under him and being dead he threw her into the pit.' This could have been useful to the Bedfords but Davis was seriously ill and expected to die, and although his surgeon thought he would make a statement, it did not happen.

Stories were also coming out of Warwick Gaol. John Mitchell, a hatter on remand for pickpocketing, said he heard Abraham Thornton say that he left Mary Ashford standing in the field and that he did not murder her but was 'the occasion of her death'.

Chapter 9

Honour

The acquittal of Thornton may have been the chief topic of conversation 'among companies consisting of both sexes' but in public the discourse about Mary and her sexual behaviour was conducted almost entirely by middle-class men. On one side were those like Edward Sadler, who was certain that it was Mary's regrettable 'lapse' that led her suddenly to take her own life, and on the other the Bedfords and Joseph Webster, who were convinced that Mary was blameless and that Thornton had raped and killed her. Then there were others, the Reverend Luke Booker the chief among them, who felt that while Mary was innocent, she had been naïve and her death was a precious opportunity to remind females of the consequences of their own ill-judged behaviour.

The debate started less than three weeks after the Warwick trial. Some men got carried away with the beauty of their arguments. In a long letter to the *Taunton Courier* on 28 August, a correspondent calling himself Philaretes wrote that, apart from Thornton, those most at fault were Mary herself and her friend Hannah. He disparaged Mary as a woman 'of an uncommonly fine figure, who dressed in a showy manner, although all her kindred are poor.' Clearly, she did not know her place and foolishly got out of her depth by dazzling Thornton with her attractions. Mary had not been robbed, nor 'killed by any blow', he wrote (as if he would know), but there were strong indications that she had been 'brutally violated' near where she was found. He thought Hannah Cox probably lied in her evidence because 'she waited, to walk back with Mary Ashford, seemingly for safeguard; yet she left her without any warning, at midnight, in the fields, alone with a man who had never spoken to her before; and who, upon his own shewing… was one of those pests of society, and scandals of our public morals, who make it their business, and their boast, to debauch every young woman that is unfortunately within their sphere of corruption.' Philaretes thought Thornton had probably previously secured the cooperation of Hannah Cox and it was possible that Mary had not called on Hannah at Mrs Butler's house at all but had changed her dress at the Tyburn before she set out along the Chester Road. 'If Thornton and Cox are really innocent, it ought (for their own sakes) to be made more clear that they are so,' he wrote.

Philaretes' eccentric nonsense was swiftly, and rightly, forgotten by the public but we can see it now for what it was: an attack on the way young working-class women lived their lives. Their personal freedoms — to walk around the countryside unaccompanied, to choose their own sweethearts, to take pride in their appearance, even to canoodle in fields if they wanted — were an affront, to the respectable classes at least. Another anonymous writer, this one calling himself A Friend to Justice, whose lengthy letter to the *Birmingham Commercial Herald* was published on 20 September, was not so easily ignored. He had looked at the trial in detail, he said, and he now had an answer to the mystery, which he offered in order to allay public anxiety. Thornton was completely innocent, he was sure of it, because it was physically impossible for him to carry out the crime: he was simply somewhere else. That left a problem. If Thornton was the only suspect and he was proved innocent, who had killed Mary?

The footsteps in the harrowed field belonged indisputably to Mary and Thornton, he wrote, and they indicated 'flight, pursuit, and struggles' which some had interpreted to show that Thornton had raped Mary and then killed her to conceal it. Far from it. A Friend to Justice reasoned that the sexual intercourse had taken place before Mary went to Mrs Butler's: if he had raped her, he would not have then let her out of his sight; he would not have let her go to Mrs Butler's, where she would 'proclaim her ravisher'; nor would he have stalked and killed her after she left Mrs Butler's because by then she would have told Hannah that she had earlier been raped. A Friend was also sceptical that a rape and murder could be carried out within forty yards of a footpath and a high road (Penns Mill Lane) and only a short distance from two cottages. Thornton's 'gratuitous' exclamation 'Why I was with her until four o'clock this morning' when Daniel Clarke informed him that Mary had been murdered and his failure to change his bloodied shirt were further proofs of his innocence. 'Would a murderer have thus disclosed the most powerful of all the facts which constitute his accusation?'

So what did happen to Mary? A Friend could not be absolutely sure but, like Edward Sadler, he speculated that 'the unhappy woman was herself the immediate instrument of her destruction'. This made perfect sense. 'I have been told that the unfortunate Mary Ashford was a young woman of unimpeachable character, and I most willingly believe that, until the time she met with Thornton, she had lived without reproach,' he wrote. That is what led to her suicide — 'the consciousness of having forfeited all that was dear to woman; a feeling which could only have existed in a mind which had previously been impressed with a strong sense of chastity.' She had '[betrayed] her own virtue to all the temptations of artful persuasions and alluring promises, of a heated fancy, and a ministering opportunity.' The proof was two-fold. The first was that she hung her head when John Humpage walked past. If Thornton had been threatening her she would have appealed to him for help and protection. The second was that she did not tell Hannah that Thornton had attempted to 'take liberties' or had detained her in the fields:

> 'What then are we to believe? that he, the ravisher of the morning, had remained with her innoxious during the night? that he had taken no advantage of the hours of darkness and solitude? that he had not so much as importuned her with one licentious proposition? Yet she makes no complaint, claims no protection, gives an untrue history of the night's adventures [she lied about staying with her grandfather], and at last fearlessly issues forth from Mrs Butler's, and exposes herself without apprehension to the peril of his attacks and outrages. There is but one possible way of accounting for such conduct, and that is, by supposing that she had previously consented to his desires.'

Warming to the scenario he had created, A Friend imagined what had happened. Thornton was an 'advantageous match' for Mary (compared with her family, his was wealthy). She may have intended to go to her grandfather's as they walked along the Chester Road but, persuaded by Thornton, she decided instead to accompany him up Bell Lane towards the foredrove. By now she was in 'a situation of peril'.

> 'The man, emboldened by the place and hour, becomes urgent in his solicitation. Possibly he engages to marry her. She resists — she escapes — is overtaken — hesitates — listens — struggles for a while; and then in an evil moment, heated by the past amusements of the evening, forgetful of the precepts she had lately revered — of her former chastity, and her now certain shame — she surrenders her virtue under circumstances of peculiar humiliation and disgust.'

It was a story similar to the 'great importunity' conjured by Justice Holroyd at the trial and very close to the theories Edward Sadler expanded on in his brief for the defence counsel. What may have appeared to be a brutal rape was nothing but the unpolished seduction of a girl from a poor family who had seen in Thornton a possible husband and had initially resisted but then got rather excited after a bit of rough handling.

After the deed, Mary and Thornton had walked together towards Erdington. At the horsepit, Thornton stopped and promised to wait for her there but when she returned, after leaving Mrs Butler's, he had gone. 'The truth is now manifest; she perceives that she is ruined and deserted. Her hopes of marriage, if she had entertained any, are now fled. She can look for nothing from Thornton but merciless exposure to gratify an unfeeling boast. A virtue so long preserved! A fall so sudden! To have been won like the harlot!' She hurried on until she reached the 'well-remembered scene of her degradation'.

'Is it incredible or even improbable, that she should take the desperate resolution of plunging into the pit, and terminating at once her earthly shame and sorrows?' asks A Friend. He did not mean to be harsh: 'I speak for justice only, and not to condemn.' Mary was in God's hands now and 'the bitterness of her death has procured her the commiseration of every feeling heart.'

Of those who took exception to A Friend to Justice's version of events, the Reverend Luke Booker, the vicar of Dudley, was the most fervent. This middle-aged, much-married clergyman (he was unlucky enough to be widowed three times) was in great demand as a preacher of instructive poems and fund-raising sermons, among them *Britain's Happiness; An Assize Sermon ... Exhibiting an Historical Review of Providential Interpositions in Favour of the British Empire* (1792), *A Sermon preached in the Parish Church of St Thomas at Dudley... and an Address to the Common People, &c. on the Subject of Riots* (1793) and *A Discourse (Addressed Chiefly to Parents) on the Duty and Advantages of Inoculating Children* (1802). A lofty socially conservative patrician whose kindness of manner towards his inferiors was said to have earned him their affection and loyalty, he saw in Mary's death a chance to correct the lax and carefree attitude of young working-class women to their personal safety.

Booker had early on contacted William Bedford to offer his support to the campaign to bring Thornton to trial once more, and he had started a fund to raise money for Mary's gravestone. He was not a man of wealth so his greatest contribution would have to be words and he set about writing a rebuttal to the fallacious allegations made by A Friend to Justice.

He made time to visit the 'melancholy scene' with Mary's grandfather, William Coleman: while they walked together to the foredrove, Coleman, in tears, talked about Mary as a child; when they stopped at the stile where Mary and Thornton were seen by John Humpage, Booker was overwhelmed with the feeling that this was a scene of 'artful seduction, on *his* part; and of invincible purity on *hers*.' Booker was sure Thornton had earlier engineered Hannah's departure in order to be alone with Mary but he also accepted that Mary may have been interested in Thornton because he was a 'man of property', that she may have 'lent a too-willing ear' to his 'artful addresses' and been 'flattered by his guileful attentions' and 'insidious artifice', and this had meant that she left it too late to call at her grandfather's. Booker's theory was that Thornton had laid in wait for Mary on her way home after Mrs Butler's. The footprints in the harrowed field were indications that a '*voluntary* surrender of her chastity was impossible,' for if it was voluntary, why did she struggle? That no such struggle had taken place before she reached Mrs Butler's was proved by her cheerful demeanour while she was with Hannah ('Don't I look like a rake!' she said while combing her hair).

Booker was particularly disturbed by A Friend to Justice's comparison of Mary to a harlot, and called on him to withdraw it. She was of unimpeachable character, he said, as proved by those who knew her, including the landlord of the Swan, where she had worked for ten years: 'She was a young woman of excellent character, particularly modest, and very industrious.' Her chastity, which was well known, was a measure of her virtue. According to the landlord, 'If anyone offered to take even the least liberty with her, he always received such a rebuff as to deter him from doing so a second time.'

As Booker saw it, Mary's fate provided a moral for his 'gentle female readers', those who were 'lovely like her, yet inexperienced'. They should avoid her fundamental mistake, which was 'going to a public amusement, where she met the author of her ruin, unattended by a discreet male relative, or a prudent matron-friend.'

Unmarried working-class women had more freedom to be outside the house than their middle-class counterparts, purely because they worked. Whether they lived with their employer or at home with their family they would routinely and regularly run errands and go to market, which required unfettered communication with male and female friends and neighbours. Mary regularly walked the seven miles or so from her uncle John Coleman's farm to stand alone in Birmingham market and sell butter and eggs. To chaperone her would have been both impracticable and wasteful — it would affect her productivity and take up the time of another working person. Middle-class men — lawyers, clerics, merchants, doctors and the gentry — certainly did not want this level of autonomy for their own unmarried daughters. Such freedom would stain their reputation and harm their chances of a good marriage; women, married or not, should always be under the control of a man.

This is not to say that unmarried women, especially those living in country villages, were not bound by traditional rules of chastity and respectability. Nevertheless, people do not always adhere to convention nor think of the consequences of transgression. It has been estimated that during this period up to forty per cent of brides were pregnant at the time of their marriage. The difference between the classes was that amongst working people this was not necessarily a reason for moral panic. If a pregnancy arose from a steady relationship which would eventually lead to marriage (even one that was not sanctified by the church), unmarried parents were granted a degree of tolerance. The poor were not always able to marry when they wanted to: there was the marriage licence to buy to start with, but a union might also involve cash outlay, for furniture, bedding, kitchen equipment and rent. It was the middle class who saw pregnancy before marriage as a disaster. For the labouring classes, it was something that usually could be discreetly managed.

Why was Mary, for her middle-class defenders, the perfect tragic female working-class victim? She was good-looking, unmarried and a virgin. After the Warwick trial journalists strayed into the superlative when describing her: 'Human form was never moulded into a finer symmetry than that which distinguished [her] person' was a much-copied sentence in the many reports and pamphlets published. Whatever Mary was actually like in life was not of great interest. Now that she was dead, she could be controlled, beatified as sweet, virtuous, humble and vulnerable, and that meant that she, or the idea of her, was properly deserving of manly chivalric protection. It put men at the centre of the story.

At this time of anxiety-inducing social unrest, when workers were increasingly agitating for political and human rights, Mary could act as a worthy working-class recipient of the middle-class's benevolent compassion for people of all ranks. To optimise Mary's acceptability as a beautiful, helpless heroine, her image was glossed up. A cameo-shaped etching began to appear in which she was shown wearing a prim high-necked frilled frock and thick coat, her beribboned bonnet framing well-behaved curls. A matching portrait of Thornton was all bovine brutishness: a sloping forehead, low-set ears, thin hair and the hint of a smirk.

There were places where Mary remained Mary: in the fairs and markets of Warwickshire a three-act play titled *The Mysterious Murder: Or, What's the*

Clock? was performed to appreciative crowds. Written by George Ludlam, who worked as a prompter at Birmingham's Theatre Royal, it featured 'Maria Ashfield'. She is a three-dimensional character, simultaneously cautious but trusting, unhappy about telling a lie to her friend 'Hannah Fox' about where she had spent the night and embarrassed to be seen in Abram Thorntree's company. It is Thornton who is reduced to a flat pantomime villain. 'I see I shall be compelled to use violence, she is so refined in her ideas,' he says while plotting the rape. The play is full of musings and whispered asides from Thorntree, who is portrayed as a man of substantial property rather than the son of a builder and farmer but much of the spoken content is a straight lift from the reports of the Warwick trial and the plot follows real events almost exactly. Sadler is represented as the corrupt and cynical 'Mr Quibble', who fabricates an alibi for Thorntree by bribing witnesses. There is even a plausible theory of mind for Thorntree — 'Had I not given way (in my childhood) to those little acts of cruelty I was permitted to pursue...'

A much later commentator pointed out that the play, published before the legal process against Thornton was exhausted, was 'entirely of an improper character, as imputing guilt to a person who had been legally acquitted, and perjury to the witnesses by whom a satisfactory alibi had been established.' In 1817 audiences did not care. *The Mysterious Murder* was hugely popular; local bookshops could not keep up with demand and Taylor, the Birmingham printer, had to reissue it several times. In the preface to the second edition, Ludlam said he was motivated to write it as a 'humble instrument of exposing the perfidy and baseness of that villain, be he whom he may,' expecting it to be 'one of those short-lived flying productions of the present day, which buzz for a short time then sink into oblivion and are seen no more.'

While *The Mysterious Murder* does not show the rape and murder, it has Thorntree removing Maria's shoes and bonnet from her dead body and the surgeon later pronouncing that Maria 'appeared to have been violated; up to this period I do not believe she had ever had connexion with man.' Genteel people found these explicit conversations disgusting, forgetting that the play was not written for them. Ordinary people understood its messages very well: that they were oppressed by unfairness and mental cruelty and that if you have enough money you can do more or less anything to poor people and get away with it. 'A poor man possesses feelings equal to a rich one's...We often see the slightest faults of the poor, punished with severity; whilst those of a more grosser nature, of the rich, pass unnoticed,' says Abram Thorntree's afflicted father who nevertheless rescues his son — and himself — from ignominy by ordering Mr Quibble the lawyer to buy off the witnesses.

Chapter 10

Habeas Corpus

On the morning of 22 October, John Bedford rode to Penns Mill Lane to ask William and Fanny Lavell to call on all the Erdington witnesses and tell them they would be required to give new depositions at his New Street office. He travelled on to see Joseph Webster and later, when he was back in Birmingham, received Paul Moon James, a Quaker banker and businessman who had become a supporter of the case against Thornton. Later that day, Bedford also squeezed in letters to the Reverend Booker and to his London agents and on the following he visited some of the new witnesses, as well as Mary's mother and uncle Charles Coleman, and wrote more letters; in the evening, he called on William Bedford and on another supporter, Josiah Robins, a surveyor and auctioneer who lived at Aston Manor. Friday 24th was spent on legal paperwork and in examining the witnesses who had come from Erdington, during which he made rough copies of their depositions. Then he called on Mr Davis, the ailing stonemason who had told his surgeon what Thornton had said to him at Birmingham Gaol ('the girl died under him') and who now denied having said anything like that. Saturday was a precious day off but on Sunday he was back at his desk, writing another letter to the Reverend Booker and, once again in the saddle, riding off to interview witnesses about the exact whereabouts of William Jennens, the Birmingham milkman, early on 27 May when he said he saw Thornton at Holden's farm.

And so it continued. Witnesses, letters, documents, consultations with his uncle. Tuesday 28 October was a turning-point, the day Bedford sent the affidavits to his London agents applying to a judge for a writ of habeas corpus (in Latin, literally 'you have the body'), the requirement to bring a prisoner before the court so that it could be determined whether or not that person was imprisoned lawfully and whether or not he should be released. The writ would require Thornton to be taken from Warwick to London to appear at the Court of King's Bench at Westminster Hall.

As ever, there was more work to do, more people to meet. That evening John Bedford received another supporter: Sir Richard Phillips, a notable reformist and the publisher of *The Monthly Magazine*, which afterwards printed an article praising the public-spirited inhabitants of Birmingham for their 'humane attention to the tragical case of Mary Ashford', and singled out William Bedford, his fellow magistrates and the local gentlemen and clergymen for their zeal in pursuing the 'real perpetrator' of the crime. The Bedfords' coterie of concerned gentlemen who could be relied on for support in the press and contributions to the legal fund was growing.

Despite this, the Bedfords must have been apprehensive about the next stage. They had extensive additional evidence but much of it was insubstantial. The best they could hope for was that the individual statements of the new witnesses, while not compelling on their own, in aggregate and in combination with the evidence already given at the Warwick trial would be enough to convince first the panel of judges to allow the case against Thornton and then, eventually, a jury to convict him.

At around this time, the Bedfords had started to hear worrying rumours that Thornton's lawyers were considering a clever legal answer to the appeal of murder that could put paid to the entire process, but they were not about to give up the fight and decided to proceed anyway.

On Monday 3 November, the writ of habeas corpus arrived at the New Street offices and John Bedford dashed off to see John Hackney, the Sheriff of Birmingham's officer, to instruct him to send it by special messenger to Warwick Gaol. By the end of the week Thornton would be in London, once more facing his accusers and contemplating his fate.

The next day, when William Bedford was at the New Street office, a packet of documents and letters was delivered to him. He read the contents almost in disbelief. Here was information that might swing everything in their favour. The clerk to Lord Sidmouth, the Home Secretary, had sent him a statement recently made by Omar Hall, who had shared a cell with Thornton at Warwick Gaol during the summer, giving details of his conversations about the rape and the murder and information about visits to Thornton by the assistant constable Thomas Dales. Hall had now been transferred to a prison hulk moored on the Thames at Woolwich, east of London, where he had fallen ill soon after arriving. When the ship's surgeon made his rounds he had taken the opportunity to declare that he wanted to make a disclosure about Thornton. The Captain alerted John Capper, the Superintendent of Prison Hulks, who personally took down Hall's statement and sent it to the Home Office.

'He confessed to have committed the rape, and said in what way it was done, which is too brutish to name,' read Hall's statement. Thornton did not admit to the murder but he came close to it: 'He never fully confessed to putting her [Mary] into the pit in a living state, altho' in all his transactions and conversations signified to me that he had done so in a dead one.' The two prisoners had discussed Thornton's chances of getting off and compared the evidence against him to other cases where prints and marks had been important, including that of Benjamin Mycock in 1812, betrayed by his footprints, and Isaac Brindley in 1816, whose patch on his corduroy breeches had done for him. Thornton was confident he would get off 'as the nails in his shoes was [sic] so small that they could not possibly make a print as any man could swear to' and in any case there could be no print of the knee of his breeches because the only time he was on his knees Mary's petticoat was under them. He had nothing to fear but Thomas Dales who had incriminating evidence against him. He told Hall that when Dales visited him at Birmingham Gaol, he promised he would keep quiet about it, and that in any case his father had agreed to pay the man off. Hall thought the evidence might be a handkerchief and blood on the cuff of Thornton's shirt.

Thomas Dales came to Warwick Gaol at the end of June and Thornton told Hall that it was because 'he [Dales] had something more to say to him' but they had not managed to finish their conversation because the turnkey had interrupted them. After Dales left, Thornton asked Hall to lend him pen, ink, paper and sealing wax, which Hall initially refused to do. It would have been a breach of the trust the Governor had put in him; the writing materials were provided so he could write on behalf of unlettered prisoners. Eventually, however, on the promise of reward once Thornton was free, he relented. He watched as Thornton wrote a letter and addressed it to Dales but was not able to see what was in it (it would have been smuggled out by a fellow prisoner about to be released). Dales visited one final time and spoke to Thornton through the turnkey's window, while Hall lurked nearby, trying to eavesdrop. He heard Dales say, just before leaving, 'I shall not want to see you again and I hope you will perform your promise on your liberty and you will find me to do the same as agreed.' On 22 July Hall was transferred to the prison hulk to await departure for New South Wales but before he left, Thornton managed a quick word; he hoped Hall would say nothing about their conversations.

As a lawyer, William Bedford knew to treat everything Omar Hall claimed with caution. His statement was tainted. Hall could have read the newspaper reports about the trial and made up the whole thing. At the same time, the statement confirmed everything that Bedford knew to be true. As Bedford believed that Dales's perjured evidence was the primary reason for Thornton's acquittal, his visits to Thornton were of the greatest interest. Before heading home he dashed off a letter to his nephew, excitedly telling him about this new development. 'You will of course consult Mr Chitty… and then go to the Secretary of State's Office, through whom you may be able to have access to Omar Hall,' he wrote. Once at home at Birches Green, he sat down to reply to Lord Sidmouth. He was suspicious about Hall's reasons for not divulging this information earlier, he wrote, but he was 'strongly induced to believe that what he has stated so far as respects Dales is true.' He wanted John Bedford to interview Hall himself and, if necessary, he had 'no doubt but your Lordship will procure him [Hall] a free pardon.' Unless this happened, as a convicted felon, Hall would be barred from giving evidence in court.

While William Bedford was considering Omar Hall's statement, Henry Tatnall, at Warwick Gaol, was served with the writ of habeas corpus concerning Abraham Thornton and consequently took his prisoner to London the following day, Wednesday 5 November. Shortly before one o'clock on Thursday he delivered him to the Court of King's Bench at Westminster Hall, the crumbling centuries-old edifice next to the Houses of Parliament. William Ashford and his uncle Charles Coleman also travelled to London for the hearing.

At this point the case began a new phase, on a new and wider stage. The failed trial of Abraham Thornton at Warwick was already notorious across the country but now that it was to be played out again, in London, it was no longer merely the sad tale of the death of a pretty country girl at the hands of a heartless village lothario. It entered the national consciousness not only as a cause célèbre but as a marker of the state of the statute book. The use of the antiquated process appeal of murder in order to right a wrong verdict gave the case an archaic cast.

The appeal of murder was an oddity, an anomaly left over from the Middle Ages, a harkening back to times when private citizens settled justice for crimes of violence themselves; it did not belong to a modern state. Nevertheless, the process was valid and William Ashford was entitled to pursue this avenue. Each stage of appeal of murder required the approval of a panel of four judges of the Court of King's Bench (Lord Ellenborough, the Lord Chief Justice, Justice Bayley, Justice Abbott and Justice Holroyd, who had been the trial judge at Warwick) before proceeding to the next. At the conclusion of a stage, one or other of the sides required time to consider and respond. This first hearing marked the opening of a slow and formal dance between the opposing legal teams.

Surprisingly, given the notoriety of the case across the country, there were few spectators at the first hearing. Newspapers had reported that Thornton would be appearing but gave no details, saying only that it would be 'in a few days'. As we shall see, every time the court convened the stakes rose, the tension ratcheted up and more members of the public arrived at Westminster Hall hoping to see Thornton in person or witness this strange legal drama. Unlike at Warwick, women were permitted to observe, much to the pursed-lipped consternation of the *Observer* on 23 November:

> 'How far it may be considered decorous to have introduced respectable females to a Court of Justice during such a proceeding, and under the circumstances of the case…our readers will be enabled to form their own judgement.'

Nathaniel Gooding Clarke, who had led the prosecution at Warwick, now appeared for William Ashford, the appellant, this time with John Gurney, a tough and experienced King's Counsel who had earned praise for the prosecution of John Bellingham, the assassin of Prime Minister Spencer Perceval in 1812, along with John Richardson and Joseph Chitty. Thornton, the appellee, was once more represented by William Reader and Henry Revell Reynolds.

In court, Thornton, wearing his black coat, showed his usual lack of concern. 'He affects to treat the affair lightly,' reported the *Public Ledger and Daily Advertiser* on 3 November, while the *Examiner,* six days later, discerned 'firmness' in his demeanour. Whatever was really going through his head, from the time of his arrest at Tyburn House by Thomas Dales Thornton appeared, in public at least, not to be worried in the least by what was happening to him.

At the hearing, he was officially given into the custody of the Marshal of the Marshalsea. Then Lord Ellenborough ordered him to be placed at the bar so that he could hear the count against him. He asked William Ashford if he would like it read aloud, to which Ashford agreed (he could not read, or at least not well), after which he signed the document with his mark. Clarke then moved that the defendant be required to plead, but here Reader interposed, saying that Thornton had not had notice of the proceedings and, pushing the bounds of credibility, that he himself had been instructed only the previous evening. 'From the rareness of cases of the kind, it was a matter that required much consideration,' he said, citing an adjournment in the case of Matthew and Patrick Kennedy, the brothers who had killed Mr Bigby on Westminster Bridge in 1769 and were subsequently rearrested on an appeal of murder. Clearly, Reader had been doing his homework while being uninstructed. Ellenborough agreed to defer the case for ten days.

Thornton was taken off to the Marshalsea, the debtors' prison on the south side of the Thames where, compared with the other inmates at least, he was accommodated in conditions of luxury. This was not the hideous institution of the eighteenth century where poor prisoners were tortured with skullcaps and thumbscrews. It had been rebuilt in 1811 but was nevertheless notoriously overcrowded and noisy. Unlike the debtors, Thornton would not have had the option to be allowed out of the prison during the day (in order to earn money to pay off debts) but was given a room usually reserved for political prisoners and allowed to take an hour's exercise in the yard and to receive visitors without restriction. Like all prisoners, he had to pay for his own food and drink and his family regularly sent remittances for this.

The next day, in his Covent Garden hotel room, John Bedford wrote to his uncle at Birches Green. He was pleased with progress in the case, 'considering that we worked in the dark.' The ancient legal process they had embarked on was as unfamiliar and worrisome to them as they hoped it would be for Thornton's side. He was relieved that the judges had researched it and that Lord Ellenborough was in general supportive of the 'mode and form' of the proceedings. The ten-day hiatus was welcome and gave him a chance to travel to Woolwich to interview Omar Hall on the prison hulk. It was imperative to hear what he had to say as soon as possible.

Before he sealed it, he scrawled a line across the top of the letter. 'All is gloom here at the melancholy fate of the poor Princess Charlotte. Prince Coburg almost frantic.' Charlotte, second in line to the throne after her father, had died shortly after giving birth to a stillborn son.

Long a favourite of the public, both for her spirited defiance of her father the Prince Regent in making her own choice of husband (she broke off a strategic engagement to the Prince of Orange and insisted on marrying the impoverished but handsome Prince Leopold of Saxe-Coburg-Saalfeld) and for her modest tastes and approachable manner (a contrast to her profligate and dissolute father), Charlotte was George III's only legitimate grandchild and thus second in line to the throne. The country immediately entered deep mourning. Shops and theatres closed. Linen-drapers ran out of black cloth. The Princess's death, said the *Morning Chronicle* on 7 November, was 'a calamity that must involve the Empire in universal doom.' Much like Mary Ashford's death had done in Warwickshire earlier in the year, the undeserved fate of the Princess served to unite people of all ranks in grief and regret.

Omar Hall, abruptly removed from Warwick Gaol in July and taken to the prison hulk *Justitia*, probably feared that he would die before he ever sailed for New South Wales. Most of his fellow prisoners were violent hardened thugs and the ship was insanitary and verminous. Within the first two months of his confinement seven men had shuffled off the mortal coil, variously dying of fever, smallpox, consumption and dropsy.

The hulks were obsolete, mastless, stationary ships, first used as prisons in 1776 when the American War of Independence halted transportation across the Atlantic and, although they were meant to be a temporary measure, they were not withdrawn until 1857. Their purpose was to provide free labour for the Woolwich naval dockyards. James Hardy Vaux, a prisoner on the *Retribution* prison hulk in the early 1800s, described the routine:

> 'Every morning, at seven o'clock, all the convicts capable of work, or, in fact, all who are capable of getting into the boats, are taken ashore...and there employed at various kinds of labour; some of them very fatiguing; and while so employed, each gang of sixteen or twenty men is watched and directed by a fellow called a guard. These guards are commonly of the lowest class of human beings; wretches devoid of feeling; ignorant in the extreme, brutal by nature, and rendered tyrannical and cruel by the consciousness of the power they possess.'

Most were moored by the Thames but there were also hulks elsewhere, including Portsmouth, Plymouth and Cork. Life aboard was miserable and possibly endless. A prisoner could be on a hulk for years before the state decided to take him or her to the opposite side of the world. The convicts dubbed life aboard 'a voyage to nowhere'.

John Capper, who had been Superintendent of Prisons and the Hulk Establishment for three years, had tried to make improvements to the food and clothing provided on the hulks and the chaplain had ensured that the prisoners had their spiritual needs met by providing bibles and services, but the regime remained harsh and the conditions horrible. At Warwick Gaol, the authorities valued Hall for his education. The Governor asked him to scribe for the other inmates and for this he was allowed to associate freely in the prison. On the *Justitia*, he was treated the same as any of the other 250 convicted felons. The change in his status combined with his illness must have tipped Hall into the decision to play his ace.

By the middle of September, Omar Hall was so ill that he was removed to the *Alonzo*, a hospital ship serving all the hulks at Woolwich, which is where John Bedford interviewed him on 7 November, having received a warrant from the Home Secretary. Bedford would have made the eastbound ten-mile journey, probably by hackney cab, passing streets pervaded by a general air of gloom and grief for the loss of the Princess and her son, where shops were draping their fronts in black, through the Kent boroughs of Southwark, Rotherhithe and Deptford to Woolwich Naval Dockyard. A ferryman rowed him over to the *Alonzo* and in a relatively quiet corner of the vessel or perhaps even in the Captain's quarters, the former banker and businessman divulged to John Bedford what Thornton had said about the rape and murder of Mary Ashford and how he had seen Thornton whispering with Thomas Dales at Warwick Gaol.

Hall's words about the rape were sickening but Bedford thought they would be of little use in a second trial of Thornton. The prosecution had lost the case at Warwick primarily because of the alibi evidence (despite his uncle's insistence that it was Dales's perjury that was to blame), not because they could not prove that Mary had been raped. What about the rest of his statement? Hall's allegations about Thomas Dales, who appeared to be blackmailing Thornton, could be useful and ought to be verified. The authorities at Warwick Gaol would be able to confirm, or not, whether Dales visited Thornton and this was where Bedford's focus now fell.

Naturally, John Bedford was on high alert for lies and untruths. Could Hall have used newspaper reports of the case to manufacture his statement? The prisoner admitted that he had read short reports about the trial but no more than that. All his information had come directly from Thornton himself, he said. Before Bedford left the ship, he urged Hall to try to remember more details of his conversations with Thornton and to write immediately if he had anything further to say. Before he left Woolwich, Bedford asked to be taken to the *Justitia*, so that he could ask the Captain which papers were taken on board and whether Hall had access to them or to information about the case from other convicts.

As Bedford sat in the *Alonzo* talking to Omar Hall, a very different drama was entering its final act. In Derby, the apparent ringleaders of the Pentrich Rising, convicted traitors Jeremiah Brandreth, William Turner and Isaac Ludlam, were drawn on a hurdle to the gallows in front of the prison, assisted up the ladder of the scaffold, hooded and hanged while a crowd of six thousand watched. After half an hour, one by one, their dead bodies were cut down and laid on a bench in full view of the public. Then they were decapitated. The spectators groaned when the executioner failed to fully separate Brandreth's head from his body with the first blow of the axe. An assistant rushed forward with a knife to complete the job and the head fell into the basket, provoking a 'burst of horror' in the crowd. 'Behold the head of the traitor Jeremiah Brandreth!' exclaimed the executioner holding it up by his black curly hair. 'Some of the women in the crowd ran away in alarm and dismay from the dismal spectacle,' reported the *Morning Chronicle* on 8 November:

> 'Some hisses and groans were heard…The panic spread like lightning, and a confused idea that the dragoons were about to charge the populace in consequence of the hisses that had escaped them, caused the immense crowd assembled in front of the prison to retire in all directions in the utmost consternation.'

On Sunday 9 November, a gravestone was placed over Mary's resting place at Sutton Coldfield church, paid for by the subscription organised by the Reverend Luke Booker, who had employed his much-praised talent for composition to write the lines of the inscription. Booker, never lacking in kind condescension, saw Mary's tombstone as a permanent tablet on which he could advertise his message to England's young females and those who were supposed to be in charge of them:

> 'As a warning to female virtue, and a humble
> Monument to female chastity,
> This stone marks the grave of
> MARY ASHFORD,
> Who, in the 20th year of her age,
> Having incautiously repaired to a
> Scene of amusement, without proper protection,
> Was brutally violated and murdered
> On the 27th of May 1817.
>
> 'Lovely and chaste as is the primrose pale,
> Rifled of virgin sweetness by the gale,
> Mary! — The wretch who thee remorseless slew,

Avenging wrath, which sleeps not, will pursue;
For, though the deed of blood be veil'd in night,
Will not the Judge of all earth do right?
Fair blighted flower, the Muse that weeps thy doom
Rears o'er thy murdered form this warning tomb.'

Booker had by now completed his riposte to the article by A Friend to Justice that had so insulted Mary's memory but had taken a decision to defer publication until after the appeal of murder against Thornton had concluded. The last thing he wanted to do was jeopardise the legal process against the destroyer of this virtuous young woman.

The Bedfords could no longer ignore the rumours about Thornton's lawyers' possible response to the appeal of murder. John Bedford, increasingly nervous, wrote to his managing clerk, George Yates, on 11 November, six days before the resumption of the hearing: 'It seems that the appellee [Thornton] has the option of waging battle and of challenging the appellant [William Ashford] to single combat, which if not accepted by the appellant, the suit is lost.' Unless they could persuade the court not to allow it, he was 'very apprehensive our poor little knight will never be able to content [sic] the battle with his brutish opponent.' Yates was of the opinion that the court would exercise discretion to 'prevent the ends of justice being defeated and the present enlightened age disgraced by so absurd a relic of Ignorance, Superstition and Chivalry,' but agreed with Bedford on the impossibility of combat between Thornton and Ashford. 'As well might a wolf and lamb be put together to fight as Thornton and Ashford.' It was essential to persuade the judges not to allow it. John Bedford urgently requested a consultation with his legal expert Joseph Chitty. The court hearing was only four days away and their side needed to find the relevant legal precedents and authorities.

At this late stage, new evidence about Thornton was still coming to light, but it continued to be scrappy and disappointing. The day before the hearing, Mr Eggington wrote to Bedford about an old pedlar woman who, when applying for poor relief after being robbed of her goods, told the overseer that William and Martha Jennens lied at the Warwick trial. The woman had seen them arguing that morning and heard William Jennens ask Thornton why his clothes were so bloody and Thornton reply that he had been bleeding sheep. Eggington tried to track her down, without success, and nothing was heard from her after that.

Chapter 11

Challenge

Early on Monday 17 November in the clear crisp air, a restless and noisy crowd gathered outside Westminster Hall, eager to see the notorious Abraham Thornton as he arrived for the hearing. They stood in the yard looking up Whitehall, straining to see Thornton's carriage as it rounded the bend of Charing Cross from the Strand. Just before eight o'clock there were shouts of 'Here he comes!' and by the time the coach, which was under military escort, reached the yard the crush was so great that few caught a glimpse of the alleged murderer. Those who did manage it would have seen a burly young man, wearing his signature black coat, drab-coloured breeches and a broad-brimmed hat, with the overall appearance, commented some newspapers, of a respectable-looking farmer up from the country.

Henry Sculthorpe, a bookbinder born in Westminster, writing in *Notes & Queries* sixty-eight years later, remembered being taken down to Westminster Yard as a six-year-old boy to witness Thornton's arrival. 'On the entry of the car into Palace Yard the soldiers simultaneously unsheathed their swords, and their united glitter in a bright morning sun appeared a splendid show to my infantile vision, and afforded me more amusement than did the subject which had drawn the soldiers together, and which at the time I scarcely understood.'

The number of people who had come to see Thornton was, to use an overworked word, unprecedented. The printer John Cooper, who had been at the Warwick trial and who later compiled one of the many reports about the case, described the doors of the court as 'almost taken by storm, and nothing but the interference of the officers prevented every part of the building from being occupied by strangers.' Justice Bayley, who arrived at ten o'clock, had great difficulty getting into the hall and had to 'contend with the almost invincible curiosity of the multitude, who had recourse to every stratagem to gain an entrance.'

It was not until eleven o'clock that counsel were able to take their places. Then William Ashford came in and was shown a place in front of his legal team, after which Thornton was brought in through a secret door. Despite being protected by one of the Marshal's men and Henry Tatnall, the keeper of Warwick Gaol, he was prevented by spectators from getting to the floor of the court, forcing his guards to push people aside. Once he was in place, the journalists started scribbling down notes. They observed that Thornton showed his usual serenity, 'as if confident in a favourable result to the proceedings' and the hint of a smile.

Mr Le Blanc, the clerk of the court, read out the count, which charged that Abraham Thornton had caused the death of Mary Ashford. Lord Ellenborough asked Mr Reader whether he had anything to move. Yes, he said, Thornton should be permitted to plead, and he was accordingly brought to the bar to do so.

'Are you guilty of the said felony and murder whereof you stand so appealed?' said Mr Le Blanc, the clerk.

Reader handed Thornton a slip of paper.

'Not guilty and I am ready to defend the same with my body.'

Reader then produced from his bag a pair of large white tanned sheepskin gauntlets, crudely fashioned mittens made as one pouch with no separate thumb or fingers and decorated around the wrist with embroidered crewel work. Thornton drew one on to his left hand, which he held up, and with his right threw the other down on the floor, a challenge for William Ashford.

The right to wage battle, a leftover from early society's belief that Heaven would grant victory to the person who had right on his side, was still a legal form of defence in an appeal of murder, and although a 'trial by battel' had not taken place for centuries the rules around it still operated. The public were used to hearing about duels of honour but that form of single combat, whose own origins were medieval, had a separate code entirely outside the legal system – indeed duels were illegal – and was almost wholly confined to the upper classes.

The last certain judicial battle in Britain was in Scotland in 1597, when Adam Bruntfield accused James Carmichael of murder and killed him in battle. There was a case in 1631 in which Charles I is thought to have intervened to prevent, and another in 1638 but no record of a battle survives. Attempts to abolish trial by battle, in the seventeenth century and twice in the eighteenth, were unsuccessful.

Looking back on this scene in 1817 in Westminster Hall nearly thirty-five years later, the lawyer, diarist and reformer Henry Crabbe Robinson, who was amongst the spectators, wrote that, 'Though we all expected this plea, yet we all felt astonishment — at least I did — at beholding before our eyes a scene acted which we had read of as one of the disgraceful institutions of our half-civilized ancestors. No one smiled. The judges looked embarrassed.' William Ashford began to come forward and was about to pick up the gauntlet when he was held back by his counsel.

'What have you to say, Mr Clarke?' asked Ellenborough. Clarke had known for days that this situation was likely to occur but his reply was weak: 'My Lord, I did not expect at this time of day, that this sort of demand would have been made…The Trial by Battle is an obsolete practice'. He went on, 'It would appear to me extraordinary indeed, if a person who has murdered the sister should, as the law exists in these enlightened times, be allowed to prove his innocence by murdering the brother also, or at least, by an attempt to do so.' The Lord Chief Justice rebuked him: 'It is the law of England, Mr Clarke, we must not call it murder.' Clarke apologised but pointed out that it would be up to the court to decide whether to permit a battle to be waged. 'It is not entirely with the appellee to decide what it shall be fit to do. The court will, no doubt, look to the person of the appellant, and seeing that he is weak of body, as it is evident, and by no means capable of combating in battle with the appellee, they will, perhaps, not permit the issue to be put upon personal contest.' Peculiarly, in a trial by battle in response to an appeal no champions were permitted.

Clarke was asking for an exemption from combat for Ashford but had no legal authorities to base this on — John Bedford and Joseph Chitty's searches in the archives had proven fruitless. This, and Clarke's underpowered response to the throwing down of the gauntlet, was probably a ploy to buy time before the next stage. Knowing that a delay suited Thornton's side too, Reader condescendingly suggested to Clarke that he put in a counterplea, an affidavit setting out all the events the prosecution alleged. Lord Ellenborough agreed.

Before the court was adjourned, to resume on Saturday, Reader managed to declare that he and Reynolds had advised the defendant to issue his challenge only 'in consequence of the extraordinary and unprecedented prejudice which has been disseminated against him throughout the country.'

The end of the hearing was as chaotic as the beginning. Thornton was taken out of the court and once more met hostility from the crowd. 'He was again the object of intense curiosity, and could with difficulty be conveyed to the carriage in which he was taken to the Marshalsea,' wrote Robinson. The gauntlet was given into the custody of the officer of the court.

Coincidentally, in 1817, another case featuring a challenge issued to the appellant was going through the courts in Ireland. Three years earlier, in

Springfield, County Westmeath in broad daylight and in front of witnesses, Thomas Clancy, an agricultural labourer, shot and killed Brian O'Reilly, a rent collector and veteran of the Marines who had served with Horatio Nelson. Clancy signed a confession and was tried at the Westmeath Summer Assizes. Because he had previously admitted the crime, the prosecuting counsel called no witnesses, but when Clancy's lawyer objected to the confession being admitted as evidence, the court ruled in his favour and refused to grant the prosecutor time to produce the witnesses. As a result, Clancy was acquitted. James O'Reilly, the brother and heir-at-law of the murdered man, appealed to the Court of King's Bench in Dublin within the allotted year and a day from the date of the trial. After much discussion and many adjournments, Clancy's lawyer advised him to offer to wage battle with the appellant.

Faced with the prospect of hand-to-hand combat between Clancy and O'Reilly, Judge Downes in Dublin squeaked in disbelief: 'Am I to understand this monstrous proposition as being propounded by the Bar, that we — the Judges of the Court of King's Bench — the recognised conservators of the public peace — are to become, not merely the spectators, but the abettors of a mortal combat? Is this what you require of us?'

'Beyond all doubt,' replied Mr Allen, counsel for O'Reilly. 'Your Lordship is to be elevated on a lofty bench, with the open air above you, the public before you, in which the combatants are to do battle till both or one of them dies.'

'Aye,' said Mr MacNally, counsel for Clancy, 'from daylight to dusk, until your Lordship calls out to us, "I see a star".'

If Clancy's trial by battle had gone ahead a piece of land sixty feet (about 18m) square enclosed with lists or palisades would have been covered with gravel and sand and strewn with rushes and a stand for the judges erected on one side. Just before sunrise, oaths against sorcery and witchcraft would be incanted and at sunrise, the court would sit. A proclamation would be made for both parties to come forward. They would have to take each other's hands and swear: the accuser that the accused did kill the deceased and the accused that he did not. They were then both to declare 'that they have about them no bone, no stone, no charm of any sort, whereby the law of the devil may be exalted, or the law of God depressed.' The opponents were to be bare-armed and bare-legged, and armed with a wooden truncheon and a square wooden shield. If the appellee lost the battle, he would be hanged immediately. If he killed the appellant or was able to keep fighting until sunset he would be acquitted. If the appellant turned 'craven' — meaning that he could fight no longer and threw in the towel — he was to be declared 'infamous' and be deprived of the privileges of a freeman. He would also be liable to pay damages to the appellee, who could never again be charged with the offence. O'Reilly v. Clancy never came to pass. Although the case had not yet concluded, by November, Clancy had agreed to withdraw his challenge, plead guilty and submit, no doubt to Justice Downes's great relief, to a sentence of transportation.

Were there grounds, as Clarke suggested, for the slightly-built William Ashford to refuse to take part in a battle with bull-necked Abraham Thornton? The anonymous 'Philo-Justitia', writing in the *Morning Post* on 20 November, did not think so, referring to the eighteenth-century legal authority William Blackstone who gave clear guidance on the qualifications for exemption from trial by battle: women (they were deemed too weak); peers of the realm (it would be degradation); priests (an affront to their sacred office); citizens of London ('foreign to their education and employment,' as Blackstone put it, meaning that they were not trained to fight and were more used to commerce); infants, that is men under twenty-one years of age (too immature); and the over-sixties, the blind and the lame (too infirm). William Ashford was twenty-three although newspapers, no doubt guessing from his weedy appearance, reported him to be seventeen. Physical weakness was not an excuse.

However, there was another way to avoid trial by battle that was not mentioned by Philo-Justitia: the court could rule that there was a 'violent presumption' of guilt. 'If the crime be notorious, as if the thief be taken with the *mainour* [in the act], or the murderer in the room with a bloody knife, the appellant may refuse the tender of battel [sic] from the appellee; for it is unreasonable that an innocent man should stake his life against one who is already half-convicted,' wrote Blackstone. William Ashford's lawyers would need to convince the four judges of the Court of King's Bench that the evidence against Thornton was so strong and that he was so obviously guilty that there was no need to fight it out in a battle. Joseph Chitty, for the appellant side, saw this as their only option.

Five days after Thornton threw down his gauntlet, the appeal resumed. 'The proceeding has excited so much public interest that all the avenues leading to Westminster Hall, as well as the hall itself, were thronged at least two hours before the usual time of opening the court,' wrote John Cooper. Lord Ellenborough's tipstaff and the keeper of Warwick Gaol again brought the prisoner in through the private door and he was placed at the bar between Reader and Reynolds. William Ashford was called on to submit his counterplea, a long document detailing the case put by the prosecution at Warwick, after which Reader asked for time to prepare an answer, which he was granted. Thornton was once again remanded to the Marshalsea, but not before Reader observed that most, if not all, the content of the counterplea had already appeared at the Warwick trial.

Indeed, there was nothing new in it at all: no mention of the information provided by the rumour-mill in Warwickshire nor of the prison disclosures made by Thornton to Omar Hall.

In Birmingham, 22-year-old Rowland Hill, in later life the brains behind the penny post but then a teacher at Hill Top, his father's school in central Birmingham, recognised that the map was the key to understanding the crime. With the assistance of his pupils and a colleague and his pupils, he surveyed the area between Erdington, Penns Mill Lane, Holden's and Shard End and designed an accurate engraved map which included a drawing of the scene of the crime, a cross-section of the pit, and a long explanatory caption. It sold for a shilling and was so popular that it was widely plagiarised. Versions of the map were adjoined to every pamphlet and trial report.

In late November, Omar Hall, by now sufficiently recovered to leave the hospital ship and return to the *Justitia*, wrote to Bedford with a few more details dredged from his memory. The Captain forwarded his letter with a note expressing his doubts about its worth, not realising how much the Bedfords valued all crumbs cast in their direction. Somehow the existence of Omar Hall's statement had leaked to the press and false reports claiming that Hall had been pardoned in order to appear in the coming trial had appeared in newspapers. They were followed swiftly with retractions. There would be no pardon for Hall until the authorities were convinced that he was truthful and that his story was of use. For the time being, he would have to stew on the prison hulk. The court would not reconvene until after Christmas, and this interlude allowed the Bedfords time to look more closely at his allegations about Thomas Dales and also to deal with the trickle of stories about Thornton still coming to them.

A brand new witness had emerged. John Collingwood, the cabinetmaker's apprentice who had been at Penns Hall during the inquest into Mary's death, told them that he had overheard a conversation between Thornton and his attorney Mr Sadler. As Thornton sat with Dales in a room in the house, Sadler had come in and said, 'Am I to do what I can for you?' and Thornton answered 'You have seen my father?' to which Sadler said, 'Yes, be sure and hold fast.' Sadler left the room and a couple of minutes later Dales and Thornton put their heads together and Collingwood heard Thornton whisper to Dales, 'Sadler says I must hold fast and by God it won't do to own to it.'

James Hope, who had previously reported a conversation with Thornton in a barley field, wrote to Bedford again. He had been talking to John Woodcock, Mr Twamley's miller, who had given evidence for Thornton at Warwick.

> 'I told him [Woodcock] that Mr Zachariah Twamley of Dudson Mill saw Mary Ashford taken out of the pit with her clothes turned up and ripped. He answered yes he knew Mr Twamley was very confident it was Thornton. I said John Wallsch [sic] said he followed Thornton up the mill till it was six o'clock and William Lawrence said the same. He said yes, Lawrence and he had many arguments about it. Lawrence was to have went to Warwick but he would not come to Sadler's time.'

It was, yet again, hearsay, like so much else they had been told, but it backed up information the Bedfords had received through the *Lichfield Mercury* editor James Amphlett in October and was confirmation, at least, that Sadler had been squeezing witness statements to fit his client's alibi.

There was also an anonymous letter alleging that Thornton had told Mr Barton the younger of Castle Bromwich that his father had paid off William and Martha Jennens and Thomas Dales, 'specifying each amount, accompanied with expressions of apprehension of ruin to his family.' On the subject of Dales, the Bedfords had heard back from John Grant, the head turnkey at Warwick Gaol, who confirmed that he had seen him in the turnkey's room, to which as an officer of the law he had access, exactly as Omar Hall had alleged:

> '[He] was leaning against the bars of the window and heaved up the green blind belonging to it and then saw Thornton walking away from it, towards the hall room in the court. He then put down the blind and Dales pulled to the window.'

Nathaniel Clarke, to prepare for Thornton's reply to the counterplea or replication as it was also known, travelled to Warwickshire in the first week of January to confer with the Bedfords and to look at the crime scene for himself. The Bedfords needed all the ammunition they could muster: they had just learned that Thornton's team had been strengthened by the addition of Nicholas Conyngham Tindal, an expert in medieval statute and a worthy match for their own Joseph Chitty.

Chapter 12

Words

In late 1817, as the stages of the appeal of murder were being played out in Westminster Hall, John Fairburn, the prolific producer of cheap song-books, chapbooks, playbills and caricatures, compiled a pamphlet about the case. *Horrible Rape and Murder!! The Affecting Case of Mary Ashford, A Beautiful Young Virgin Who Was Diabolically Ravished, Murdered, and Thrown in a Pit* was a mix of trial report, articles and letters culled from newspapers, including the *Lichfield Mercury*, as well as the now obligatory map. The pamphlet concluded with portraits of Mary and Thornton in oval-shaped vignettes, also lifted from other publications, and a 114-line elegy.

One of the anonymous contributors to the *Lichfield Mercury* stories (possibly James Amphlett, the editor) had been to the crime scene and talked to some of the witnesses, including William Lavell, whom he found leaning on the gate to the footpath, near what was now referred to as 'the violation tree'. Lavell spoke with affection of Mary: 'She was a very steady girl,' he said. 'One hardly ever saw her out. She was as fine a straight upright person as you ever saw, and was always a mighty brisk walker.' The letters A and T with a crude gallows had been carved in the bark of the tree where the shape of a human had been seen in the grass. This had been done by 'someone from Birmingham' said Lavell. Apparently, the site was now a destination for tourists.

A new three-act play based on the case and selling for a shilling and sixpence was published in January 1818. Unlike George Ludlam's work, *The Murdered Maid, Or, The Clock Struck Four!!!*, by an anonymous 'professional gentleman', was lumbering, dragged down by its worthy purpose; to warn young women of the dangers waiting for them should they venture unaccompanied into the world. To evade the risks of a libel suit, the setting had been moved across the Channel and the main characters given frenchified names – but it was not enough to entertain audiences. The author's promise to omit 'every disgusting circumstance' of the case on which it was based did not add to the play's appeal. It was performed at the

Sunderland Theatre in March and in Hull at the end of 1819 (probably in a shortened form), and then sank without trace.

Who wrote it? The author signed the preface only as 'S.N.E.', but it is possible that he was the Reverend Luke Booker, the righteous Vicar of Dudley who had shown such great support for Mary Ashford's cause. His pamphlet in answer to A Friend to Justice was still on hold until the appeal of murder had concluded so perhaps impatience to disseminate his moral advice to the young women of England got the better of him and he chose a fictional format to get his message out.

In London, Thornton was still held in the Marshalsea. The *Observer* newspaper, which had begun to take a great interest in the case, reported that he could occasionally be seen at the window of his room shouting down to fellow prisoners in the yard.

When the process resumed on Saturday 22 January, it was clear that the public fascination with Thornton had not diminished. Yet again, vast numbers gathered outside Westminster Hall hoping to bag a seat or at least catch a glimpse of him. To avoid the disgraceful scenes at earlier hearings, the authorities had arranged for Thornton to arrive early, before the crowds gathered; the tipstaffs discreetly took him through a passage in New Palace Yard. He was the same as ever; coolly serene, as if 'perfectly unconscious of the odious situation in which he stands.' When proceedings began, his counsel, Reader, announced that he was ready with his replication to the counterplea which, after being sworn, was handed to the clerk, who then read its 5,500 words out loud.

Reader and Reynolds had decided to include new detail about the route Thornton took to reach home. It was nearly two miles from the pit to Holden's farm but across trespass land in a straight line only one and a half (although the going would have been more difficult as there were numerous hedges and fences to climb over). If he had taken this route, as William Ashford's side alleged, he would have passed Holden's farm much later than 4.30am or so, when the milk people swore that they saw him. There was also much emphasis on Joseph Webster and William Twamley's assessment of the clocks at Mrs Butler's house and at Holden's and the fact that Thornton had not changed out of his clothes when he got home to Castle Bromwich, which was presented as a sign of innocence. Thornton utterly refuted the charge and repeated his plea to wage battle with William Ashford.

Now it was Clarke's turn to ask for time to reply, to which Reader stated he had no objections. Lord Ellenborough asked the parties to return five days later for the next stage, known as the demurrer, a plea that even if the appellant's facts are as he says, they still do not support his case. At the end of the hearing, as Thornton climbed into the waiting hackney coach to return to the Marshalsea, the crowd hissed and booed him. The *Observer* reported that this was the first time he looked shaken.

When the parties returned to court on 29 January, William Ashford's side said that Thornton's replication was 'wholly insufficient' and prayed judgment of the court that he may not be permitted to wage battle. At this, Reader announced that Thornton 'joined issue' on the demurrer, and the next date for the hearing was agreed, on 6 February, when arguments for both sides would be heard. On this date, Chitty gave what was generally agreed to be a 'learned disquisition', drawing in numerous legal precedents and also arguing that there was a prima facie case against Thornton, strong enough to deprive Thornton of a right to trial by battle. Thornton's case was based on alibi evidence. If it was as solid as he claimed it to be, why was he not confident to put it to a jury? The proceedings were adjourned for two days, when Tindal would reply.

The sitting on 8 February was spent hearing Tindal's rejoinder. It was Thornton's undoubted right to wage battle, he said, and Chitty's counterplea had failed to show that the case qualified for any of the exemptions allowed. The allegations against Thornton were vague and unanswerable — there was no violent presumption of guilt — and the appellant therefore had no case. Even if the court accepted the counterplea, Thornton's replication had sufficiently answered it. Tindal's speech lasted the entire day, at the end of which Reader asked that Thornton be granted bail. However, no sureties were in place so this was not possible and the prisoner was once more remanded back to the Marshalsea.

The *Observer*'s coverage of the appeal was especially detailed (it gave nearly two whole pages of dense text to Tindal's rejoinder to Ashford's demurrer) and it also published a sketch of Abraham Thornton at the bar on the front page of the 8 February issue. This was truly unusual and a landmark in newspaper history. The *Observer*'s only other illustration that year was of the Pentrich traitor Jeremiah Brandreth, published with a report on his execution. Newspapers rarely published pictures and the decision to portray Thornton would not have been made lightly. It was expensive and time-consuming to roll the newssheets through the press twice, first for letterpress and again for the copperplate, but Thornton was the man of the moment and the public across the country, not just those who made their way down to Westminster Hall for the hearings, were keen to see what he looked like.

Seven months previously, the murder of Mary Ashford was the only subject of conversation in Warwickshire amongst people of all classes and both sexes. Now, in London the climax of the appeal of murder and the real possibility of hand-to-hand combat were the talk of the town. At a dinner given by the Danish ambassador's residence in London Richard Rush, the American 'minister', discussed it with celebrated chemist Sir Humphrey Davy, who described the case as 'a legal burlesque' and fantasised that the parties should fight it out in a ring while Parliament and the judges looked on. Rush thought that the case was in danger of converting the Court of King's Bench into a 'theatre for prize fighting'. In all the clever chat, Mary Ashford the person had completely disappeared from view.

This was not true for everyone. In the middle of March John Bedford received a letter from John Hiscox, a London attorney, who said he had been 'roused to a phrenzy' by the case and informed him that for the sake of public justice he was working on a new pamphlet about it. To complete it he needed a correct transcript of Thornton's defence statement — or at least information on whether Thornton claimed he had reached home at any particular time — plus accurate distances between Holden's farm, Twamley's Mill, Castle Bromwich and Shard End. He enclosed some of his preliminary calculations, in which he compared true time to local time for all locations and accurate distances between the relevant locations.

The male editors of *The Ladies' Monthly Museum*, a magazine for genteel women, decided to focus on Mary in the issue of 7 March 1818, determining that their readers would be more interested in her person and life than in the tedious intricacies of the appeal of murder. In a conscious departure from their usual custom of presenting an article on a woman distinguished 'either by the splendour of her rank, or the lustre of her talents' they featured instead the 'lovely and unfortunate' Mary Ashford. They went to 'considerable pains…and some expense' to procure a likeness, publishing an engraving by John Thompson from a new painting by John Partridge showing a sweet-faced Mary bareheaded, wearing unfeasibly fashionable dress. Clearly inspired by Luke Booker's graveyard eulogy to Mary, the magazine lavished praise on 'this sweet flower, so early and so cruelly blighted' and repeated the over-the-top description of her that had appeared in numerous publications after the Warwick trial: 'A skilful sculptor might have selected her form as a model for Venus; her finely turned limbs seemed polished by the hand of symmetry; and a rare union of expression and sweetness with regularity of feature, rendered her countenance as beautiful as her figure was perfect.' Her disposition was 'open and ingenuous' with 'an affectionate heart and an amiable temper'. In deference to the feelings of their readers, the story included no details of the rape which were not '[consistent] with delicacy to state'.

On 16 April crowds once more congregated at Westminster Hall to see Thornton brought to court for the seventh time. He did not appear to be suffering in prison. The *Observer* noted on 19 April that he looked 'extremely well, and his appearance generally was that of a man whose mind was perfectly at ease.'

The case was nearing the endgame. A decision on whether the trial by battle would be granted was likely to be announced at this hearing and for this reason members of the Ashford family had travelled down to London. Two of William Ashford's aunts were admitted to court through a side door used by barristers and, not realising who he was, took seats near to Thornton. They were about to start up a conversation with him when one of the ushers asked Thornton if these women were friends of his. 'No, they are no friends of mine,' he said, half smiling. They were quickly moved off to another part of the court.

Richard Rush, the American ambassador, was in court to see for himself this 'mode of trial for dark ages'. The judges had given him the privilege of sitting with them on the bench, from which he looked down on 'about seventy' lawyers, all in wigs and gowns. He was simultaneously incredulous that in 'the highest tribunal of the most enlightened country in Europe' he was listening to a discussion about trial by battle and impressed by the seriousness with which the issue was being treated.

Joseph Chitty made valiant efforts to save the case by once more asserting that trial by battle was unnecessary because the counterplea presented a strong case against Thornton. An alibi was a perfectly proper defence for a jury to consider, he said, but trial by battle was a method of terminating a prosecution only to be resorted to when there was an absence of evidence. He began to read the counterplea and to comment on the facts in it, but Justice Bayley grew impatient. There was nothing to prove that Thornton was in Mary's company after Humpage had seen them together at the stile in the foredrove and no evidence to prove that the 'connection' did not take place before Mary went to Mrs Butler's house to change her clothes, he said. All of the marks in the field could have been made before Mary returned to Erdington and she could have died in any one of many ways: by throwing herself in the pit or by falling into the water when she went to wash herself.

Judge Holroyd, the Warwick trial judge, had some points to make on Thornton's guilt or innocence. There was no single suspicious circumstance, he said, which might not have taken place before Thornton and Mary parted and before she went back to Mrs Butler's house. Indeed, if everything alleged against Thornton happened before Mary went to Mrs Butler's, what motive did he have for lying in wait and killing her on her way home?

Lord Ellenborough consulted the other three judges for about fifteen minutes and then delivered the decision:

> 'The discussion which has taken place here, and the consideration which has been given to the facts alleged, most conclusively show that this is not a case that can admit of no denial or proof to the contrary; under these circumstances, however obnoxious [sic] I am myself to the trial by battle, it is the mode of trial which we, in our judicial character, are bound to award. We are delivering the law as it is, and not as we wish it to be, and therefore we must pronounce our judgment, that the battle must take place.'

After Lord Ellenborough stated that final judgment would be delivered in four days' time, the court rose.

Thornton was elated and it showed on his face. He 'seemed to feel a natural exultation — he seemed to quit the court in high spirits,' wrote John Cooper. Outside, the crowd was appreciably subdued.

Early on Monday 20 April another 'immense crowd' gathered at Westminster Hall to hear the delivery of the final judgment. The rumour mill had been busy: many of them believed that William Ashford would, at this late stage, take up Thornton's challenge. They were soon disabused. John Gurney stood and announced that in view of the judges' decision he had nothing further to pray. Reader then said that the appellant must either accept battle or the appellee would go free. Ashford was called, but Gurney declared that he did not propose to object to Thornton's discharge provided that no action would be taken against his client and Reader assured him there was no intention of that. In a final flourish, the court decreed that before Thornton could be dismissed he must be arraigned at the suit of the Crown to which he pleaded *autrefois acquit* (previously found innocent), so for the third time he was charged with the murder of Mary Ashford, to which he pleaded Not Guilty. Reader put in a copy of his trial at Warwick, which Sir Samuel Shepherd, the Attorney-General, declared to be correct, after which the Lord Chief Justice formally delivered the final judgment, that 'the defendant be discharged from this appeal and that he be allowed to go forth without bail.' Thornton bowed to the judges and, at Lord Ellenborough's suggestion, left the court by the private door behind the bench. At that moment, the spectators surged towards him and were held back by officers of the court.

It was over. There were no more ways to bring Thornton to justice. Once he had paid the bill for bed and board that he had run up in custody, he was free to return home and resume his old life. His enemies and the outraged public were in no mood to forgive, however, and he was sufficiently nervous of his safety to delay his return to Warwickshire for nearly two weeks. When someone recognised him as he was about to board a coach home at the Castle and Falcon in Aldersgate Street people began to insult and deride him. The *Times* discovered that he broke his journey at Coventry ('wishing to avoid public attention, [he] took a circuitous route across the Park') before taking another coach on to Birmingham.

Three weeks after Ellenborough's judgement, almost a year after Mary Ashford's body was pulled from the marl pit near Penns Mill Lane, the London stage provided the cathartic ending that the Court of King's Bench could not deliver: a return to the Middle Ages, the sight of actual hand-to-hand combat and the death of the villain. The management of the Royal Coburg Theatre (these days known as the Old Vic), which had just opened on the south side of the Thames in the dank, crime-ridden area known as Lambeth Marsh, had planned a sensational inaugural billing that included the 'grand Asiatic ballet' *Alzora and Nerine* and a splendid harlequinade, but it was the 'entirely new melo-dramatic spectacle' *Trial by Battle; or, Heaven Defend the Right* by William Barrymore and featuring new music, scenery, costumes and decorations that they were relying on to pull in the crowds.

Barrymore removed the story from its mundane Warwickshire setting. The action took place in a world of castles and gothic interiors. He also exaggerated the social differences between Mary and Thornton, who were transformed into Geralda, a simple country girl, and the evil Baron Falconbridge. The plot had Falconbridge abducting Geralda and killing her father, with her brother taking up the challenge to Falconbridge, whose knights abandon him, leaving him to fight the duel himself. In the final tournament sequence Falconbridge is killed. The *Huntingdon, Bedford and Peterborough Gazette* reported that the 'scenes were throughout well executed, and the performances are passable. The house was crowded to excess, and the pieces met with a good reception.' For the theatre audiences lost in the fantasy of the evening justice was served at last. The production ran initially for fifteen nights (and was repeated from time to time in 1818), and was still being sporadically performed in provincial theatres as late as the 1860s.

Trial by Battle was not the only melodrama based on the case to open in London. *Chateau Bromege; or, The Clock Struck Four* was performed at the Regency Theatre. A playbill describes it as based on 'melancholy fact'. Like *The Murdered Maid*, the action takes place in France, where Mary becomes Maria and Thornton Thornville, but it lacked a violation scene and there was no final judgment. Its run was short-lived.

The reaction to the failure of the appeal in the neighbourhood of Birmingham was muted. One or two sentences in local newspapers gave the bare outline of fact: that the appellee was entitled to wage battle. William and John Bedford's disappointment must have been immense, to say nothing of the feelings of the Ashford family, who on paper at least were faced with ruin. We can be confident that William Bedford and his gentlemen friends paid the court costs; a widely advertised subscription fund may also have yielded funds.

With the end of the case, the Reverend Luke Booker was finally able to publish *Moral Review of the Conduct and Case of Mary Ashford*, sixty-four pages of 'admonitory lesson to young women; deterring them from repairing to scenes of amusement, unsanctioned and untended by proper protection.' He hoped that it might be read by fathers to their daughters and brothers to their sisters. Between the lines of quoted poetry, Booker tore into the allegations made by A Friend to Justice and derided his credulity in believing in Thornton's alibi. He cited the 1812 case of Benjamin Mycock, with its reliance on footmark evidence and other circumstantial evidence and expanded on the dangers of relying on estimated time. The evidence of Mary's struggle with Thornton was 'positive proof that [she] did not degrade her character.' He thought it easy enough for the murderer to slacken his pace after running from the scene to give the appearance of strolling so as to fool witnesses, implying that the Jennens, who swore that Thornton had walked slowly past them, had been mistaken or lying.

After his return home Abraham Thornton lived with his parents at Shard End. Ostracised by his peers and neighbours, he spent his time underemployed and depressed. On 9 July his 58-year-old father died of consumption at Shard End and was buried in a corner of Castle Bromwich churchyard. His death, thought by many to have been hastened by anxiety over his son, was marked in local newspapers, who pointedly described him as a man of 'the strictest integrity, and greatly esteemed by all his neighbours and acquaintances.' A late nineteenth-century historian reported that his gravestone bore an inscription 'clearly indicative of his having died broken-hearted'. His wife Sarah and daughter Mary Line inherited everything. His son was not mentioned in the will.

The case may have been lost and Thornton set free, but the flow of words about Thornton, and his guilt or innocence, continued unabated. In reply to Booker's *A Moral Review*, A Friend to Justice published a pamphlet of his own. In *Wager of Battle: Thornton and Mary Ashford; or An Antidote to Prejudice* he expanded on his theory that Mary had thrown herself into the pit. He begged for a 'cool and quiet examination' of the circumstances rather than 'involuntary goings astray of the mind'. Appeal of murder was an 'absurd and dormant' instrument, he said, a leftover from the days of barbarity and superstition, which should never have been considered and William Ashford had been imposed on by the Bedfords, 'the deceptive bubble in the current', and 'worked into an infatuated belief' that Thornton was guilty. A Friend emphasised his credentials as an unbiased spectator at the hearings at Westminster Hall and asserted that he was not personally acquainted with Thornton. He pledged to use the profits from the publication to buy an annuity for Thornton's mother. Her husband's 'little property has been entirely consumed in his [Thornton junior's] defence,' he wrote.

Devoid of embarrassment, A Friend made the astonishing assertion that:

> 'The virgin female…seldom, nay, never, yields consent without much previous solicitation — backwardness, and at least apparent reluctance, however well-disposed she may be towards the individual to whom she either intends, or ultimately does, surrender her person.'

The words 'yield' and 'surrender' along with 'taking' and 'having' was the language of libertinism, shot through with militaristic euphemisms of conquest and calling to mind Thornton's alleged words when he saw Mary at the dance: 'I've had her sister three times. And I'll have her tonight, if I die for it.'

John Hiscox, who had earlier pressed John Bedford for information about distances and timings, published *An Investigation of the Case of Abraham Thornton Who was Tried at Warwick, August 8, 1817, for The Wilful Murder and then Afterwards Arraigned for the Rape, of Mary Ashford* using only 'An Attorney at Law' to identify himself. The pamphlet was an answer to the arguments — 'air-built castles' — of A Friend to Justice. Like A Friend, he stated that his mind was free of bias and his researches were made only in order to reveal the truth.

Hiscox focused on the issue of Thornton's alibi – 'No man can at all times remember where he was at any given time or recollect the exact time he was at a given place.' For this reason, even if a person is innocent, an alibi cannot be relied on. He was the only one to analyse and challenge A Friend's theory that Mary had committed suicide because she was so ashamed of having had sex with Thornton. To his mind, sex before marriage was not so heinous — Mary's family and friends would have forgiven her — and self-murder in such circumstances was rare. Those suicides that occurred were committed by educated women whose minds had an 'exquisite sensibility, chiefly arising from subsequent cruelty or desertion.' Genteel women simply had more to lose. Perhaps he was thinking of Lavinia Robinson throwing herself into the Irwell in 1814 after her fiancé accused her of 'a lack of chastity'. Faced with the emotional pain of abandonment and inevitable social humiliation, she became severely depressed. As for Mary, quite apart from the fact that suicide made no psychological sense, there was physical evidence to disprove it. There were no female footprints near the pit. How would she have reached the pit if not by walking?

It was A Friend's assertion that a virgin female never 'yields consent without much previous solicitation' that Hiscox found the most objectionable. Mary's earlier behaviour while she was with Thornton showed that she had been careful to avoid impropriety: she had kept to the main roads and did not enter the fields. Humpage's evidence did not prove she was in the fields, only that he thought he saw and heard a man and a woman there.

The main feature of Hiscox's pamphlet was the six pages of tables giving all the various options for routes for Thornton from the pit, with columns of 'village time' and 'real time' and calculations that would disprove Thornton's alibi, but in the end the issue of Thornton's guilt boiled down to this: his defence was not a positive alibi but an assumed one, founded on doubtful data. Jennens did not know the time — he only swore it was about half past four 'as near as he could judge'. He and his wife gave vague and uncertain estimates of the time and neither of them could say which direction Thornton had walked from; and neither could Holden junior say what time it was. Hiscox was scathing about Heydon's evidence. The gamekeeper was one of Thornton's friends.

PART 3

Chapter 13

Aftermath

When Sir Samuel Shepherd, the Attorney-General, left the Court of King's Bench after the end of the appeal of murder, he hurried back to the House of Commons and announced that he would soon be bringing in a bill to abolish both trial by battle and appeal of murder. It had been forty-three years since Parliament had last considered repeal. On 29 April 1774, a Bill for the Administration of Justice in Massachusetts Bay, a response to the dramatic destruction of tea in Boston harbour, was before committee and John Dunning, the MP for Calne, rose to support the retention of these apparently obsolete instruments. Some had objected to appeal of murder because it was a remnant of barbarism and Gothicism, he said, but 'The whole of our Constitution, for aught I know, is Gothic.' Perhaps Dunning was not being entirely transparent about his motives: beneath his witticism was a strategic opposition to any legislation affecting the colonies that differed from the 'motherland'. He need not have been so scrupulous — just over two years later the American colonies declared they were going their own way.

It is ironic that opposition to Shepherd's bill, whose journey through the parliamentary stages started in early 1819 came not from conservatives seeking to maintain the status quo but from radicals and reformers. Sir Francis Burdett, the controversial MP for Westminster and supporter of universal male suffrage, opposed it on its second reading, objecting that appeal of murder should be retained as a necessary protection from 'an undue exercise of the power of the Crown in pardoning persons convicted of murder'. Nevertheless, by June the bill reached the House of Lords, where it passed without opposition and the Prince Regent granted royal assent on 17 July 1819.

Across the country, the atmosphere of dissent and danger had not abated. A month after the repeal sixty to eighty thousand protesters, many of them women, many of them cotton loom weavers of Lancashire, who had gathered in St Peter's Fields in Manchester were addressed by the Radical

Henry Hunt. Between eleven and fifteen people were killed in the ensuing melee, with hundreds wounded. James Wroe, the editor of the *Manchester Observer*, coined the name 'Peterloo Massacre'.

The public was still troubled by the Thornton case. There were rumblings of criticism of Justice Holroyd's handling of the Warwick trial. His son Edward Holroyd felt that something should be said in his father's defence and also that a caution against the 'danger of pressing presumptive evidence too far' was timely. He had been at the Warwick trial and, having taken 'careful notes', he was at pains to point out omissions in other published accounts of the trial. He certainly had high claims for his own: his *Observations Upon the Case of Abraham Thornton, Who Was Tried at Warwick, August 8, 1817, for the Murder of Mary Ashford*, which appeared in 1819 and went into two editions, was 'the only true and authentic account yet published'. He included a new and more detailed version of the map.

There was no doubting where Edward Holroyd stood on the case. Thornton's behaviour was 'very atrocious' and there were numerous suspicious circumstances around the death of Mary that would naturally lead the public to think him guilty but they did not amount to proof. The verdict returned by the jury at Warwick was the correct one. He doubted that Mary's death was murder and he did not think it was suicide, because Mary had shown no signs of despondency and despair. He felt that a person considering suicide would not have carefully arranged her belongings by the pit — she would not have cared what happened to them — nor would she have been cheerful when speaking to Hannah at Mrs Butler's, nor walked on with such speed up Bell Lane. An altogether different scenario was more likely, he wrote. While passing through the field she noticed that she had bled onto her new white shoes. She was extremely tired after all the walking she had done; she had been awake for at least twenty-four hours, had eaten little or nothing in that time, was menstruating, and had exerted herself by having sex with Thornton in the field earlier. While standing at the edge of the pit, at the top of the bank, she stooped or turned while changing into her boots, took a step backwards, and perhaps in a faint or dizzy spell, tumbled down into the water. Why her shoes were lined up next to the bundle on the bank of the pit he does not say.

As for the state of her body, there were no marks on it apart from those that might have been made 'by consent after considerable earnestness, exertion and importunity' when she had sex with Thornton earlier that morning and the same was true of the marks on the ground near the pit. There was nothing to prove or even indicate rape. As for the trail of blood and absence of her footprints near the pit, these had a logical explanation. Thornton had not carried her body — the falling of the dew had erased her footmarks.

Edward Holroyd did accept that the marks in the harrowed field were signs of 'flight and pursuit' but again this did not equate to rape. Mary had tried to get away from Thornton, but after her initial resistance had 'yielded, a yielding obtained most probably reluctantly, and by artifice, promises, oaths, and urgent importunity, to which by her own extreme imprudence in remaining alone with a man, especially one so shortly known to her, all night in the fields, she was unfortunately exposed.' Even if she resisted, it was not rape, because she should have known better than to be in Thornton's company and to lead him to expect sex and, in any case, had given in to him.

Holroyd did not question Thornton's alibi, for which there were seven witnesses whose evidence corroborated each other; their testimony made it impossible for him to have murdered Mary. Because Thornton had named or mentioned these people in his statement, which was taken on the day of Mary's death, he would not have had time to suborn them or set up a false trail. That he was happy to come along when he was apprehended by Daniel Clarke, the keeper of Tyburn House, and freely admitted that he had been with Mary 'until four in the morning' were strong indications of his innocence.

Ten years after he tried Thornton at Warwick, George Sowley Holroyd was severely criticised in the radical press for his conduct in a gruesome child murder case heard at the Old Bailey. William Sheen was indicted for beheading his infant son. There was no doubt about his guilt, but the indictment failed because the boy had been misnamed in the paperwork. There was confusion as to his forenames, but crucially, in the opinion of Holroyd, he was referred to by the wrong surname. A second trial, in which Sheen was arraigned on thirteen alternative counts in order to identify the child, also failed on the same basis and Sheen walked free. In a long and angry editorial about the stupidity of the law, the *Examiner* reminded its readers that Holroyd was 'the Judge under whose direction Abraham Thornton was some few years ago acquitted of rape and murder, to the astonishment of the civilized world.' A year later ill-health forced Holroyd to retire from the bench. He died at his home in Berkshire in 1831.

After the ending of the case, the protagonists returned to their old routines and life continued. William Ashford went back to Hints to resume his occupation as an agricultural labourer. He married and eventually moved to Birmingham where he worked as a fish seller. His parents remained in Erdington, Ann dying in 1834, aged sixty-three, and Thomas in 1842 at seventy-two, probably while living in the workhouse at Erdington Green, where he was listed as resident in the 1841 census.

At least one of Mary's siblings, Joseph, who was six in 1817, named a daughter after her. Her sister Phoebe, whose mistress tried to break the news of Mary's death to her gently, grew up and married William Lovett, and survived to 1875. Her death was reported in the local newspapers only because of her famously murdered (and still remembered) sister. Of Ann, the elder sister who Thornton claimed to have 'had' three times, nothing is known for certain. Was she the fifty-year-old Ann Ashford recorded as living in the hamlet of Witton near Erdington in the 1841 census? Or did she decide to flee the reputation Thornton imputed to her and sail to one of Britain's colonies? Mary's friend Hannah Cox married Benjamin Carter in April 1823 in Nuneaton. William Lavell continued to live in Bell Lane until he died in 1850 at the age of sixty-nine. His colleague Joseph Bird died aged fifty-two in 1838.

A person called Thomas Dale appears in the 1822 criminal register for Warwickshire, sentenced to four months imprisonment for larceny. He could be the Thomas Dale listed in the 1851 census as a servant to an innkeeper in Rowington, but we cannot be sure that either of these is Thomas Dales.

Omar Hall, whose evidence held so much promise but was not in the end utilised, achieved his wish and was granted a free pardon, but not until December 1819, well after the end of the case. He married for a second time in 1824 and again in 1833, dying in Baswick, Staffordshire in the same year.

William Bedford moved to Batheaston where he died in 1832 at the age of seventy-eight. His nephew John, who had done the legwork for the appeal of murder, married Catherine Fitzhardinge Jenner, the daughter of Edward Jenner, the pioneer of inoculation, in 1822. After a career as a solicitor and magistrate he died in 1854 at the age of seventy.

After years of keeping his wire-drawing business from going under, Joseph Webster eventually pulled it clear of debt. With the help of his trusted manager John Bird, he started to experiment with the production of high-manganese steel. The company expanded and he made a fortune. Bird died in 1834, a major loss of expertise to the company. Joseph died in 1856 at the age of seventy-three.

The memory of the unavenged murder of Mary Ashford lived on in literature. Influenced by the appeal of murder, Sir Walter Scott included trial by battle in *Ivanhoe* (published in 1820), which was set in medieval times, in which Wilfrid fights Brian de Bois-Guilbert in defence of Rebecca.

Six years later, the case was still a topic of conversation. At a dinner with the Duke of Wellington and the Prime Minister Lord Liverpool, Robert Peel almost convinced Scott of Thornton's innocence.

The brutality shown to Mary became a marker against which other murders of women were compared. On 26 May 1827, exactly ten years after Mary had danced at Tyburn House, Mary Ann Lane, a married woman, attended a christening party given by a family for whom she had wet-nursed at Harbury in Warwickshire, thirty miles from Erdington. At the end of the evening, she left in the company William Miller, a labourer, who was walking home in the same direction. The next day her body was found in a pit. In a damp ditch nearby, there were several impressions of shoes, some of which showed a nail in the heel lying diagonally; it was compared to Miller's and found to match exactly. A yard from the pit, in the ground, there were indications of two people struggling and the mark of a knee, which was found to correspond with Miller's breeches. The clay was dug out of the soil and presented at Miller's trial at Warwick three months later. Miller made a confession and was hanged. The *Exeter Flying Post* said the case was 'in many respects, similar to that of Abraham Thornton and Mary Ashford'.

After his father's death, Abraham Thornton decided to leave England and emigrate to America, which had been his intention after his acquittal at Warwick. In early September 1818, he booked a berth on the *Independence* bound for New York but had to leave the ship when other passengers discovered his identity and objected. Later in the month he managed to board the *Shamrock*, perhaps by assuming a false name, and sailed from Liverpool. Within weeks, newspapers were publishing a bizarre rumour that he had left behind a confession. The story was that while he was in Liverpool, waiting to sail, he tried to persuade a prostitute he had befriended to go with him to America, and that he told her that the truth about Mary Ashford's death would be known soon after he left England. While he was asleep she took the opportunity to steal his papers, including a letter to the Constable of Birmingham, which she handed to Mr Blackstock, clerk to the Magistrates of Liverpool. In the letter Thornton confessed to raping Mary and said he had not intended to murder her but she persisted in saying she would expose him so he dragged her to the pit and held her under the water. The story was flatly denied by Mr Blackstock and denounced as 'a vile fabrication'. The newspapers printed retractions.

In the decades after the case ended, the fate of Thornton continued to fascinate readers. In November 1820, the *Warwickshire Advertiser* stated that he had died — it was wishful thinking. Seven months later, in a paragraph headed 'Promiscuous', the *Liverpool Mercury* said he was in America and very much alive. In 1834, he was reported to be married, 'carrying on a successful business' and vehemently denying any participation in Mary's murder. He was even thinking of returning to England. In 1861 the *Birmingham Daily Post* claimed that it had seen letters he wrote to relatives in Castle Bromwich dated up to 1831 in which he describes himself as married with a family and living a good life. Among the documents in Birmingham Archives is an unattributed newspaper clipping dating from the 1880s which says that when Thornton reached America he made a living as a pedlar and used his profits to buy several fishing boats, from which he made a fortune. It goes into some detail, all of it unsourced: he bought an estate called Black Hawk Hall, married and had a son and a daughter. The former was killed in the American civil war, and the latter died from consumption. There was a rumour that a box kept sealed during his lifetime was broken open after he died and inside were found letters and papers which indicated that Thornton had indeed been guilty of Mary's death. No one has been able to verify these assertions.

We will never know for sure what happened to him. However, a tantalising possibility about his life after he left England has been ignored for decades, hidden in the 24 August 1889 edition of the *Boston Guardian*. In a paragraph headed 'Accused People Live Long' it claimed that a few years after an article in a Birmingham newspaper referred to Thornton as the murderer, a letter arrived at the proprietor's office. Thornton, long thought dead, threatened him with a libel suit and pointed out that he had never been convicted. The article stated that Thornton claimed to have moved from America to Australia 'where he was understood to have made his pile'.

Indeed, the case was well known across the English-speaking world, The American jurist Oliver Wendell Holmes discussed it with 'two ladies of my household' in 1887. 'He may be living near us, for aught that I know,' he told them. Holmes was struck by the coincidence that just after he mentioned the case he received a letter from England in which Frederick Rathbone, a well-known dealer in porcelain and eighteenth century art, enclosed a copy of a pamphlet on 'Wager of Battel'.

As time went on and detailed knowledge of the case faded from memory, Thornton's innocence dominated over Mary's innocence. None of the public had access to Omar Hall's statement, which steadily gathered dust among papers held by Croxhall and Holbeche, the Sutton Coldfield solicitors instructed by the Bedfords. In general, it was only the people of Erdington who persisted in the belief that Thornton had murdered Mary. In any case, by the middle of the century, the primary interest of the media was no longer in the crime against her. It was the dramatic end of the age of chivalry that captured their attention. Numerous stories about the case were published in *Notes & Queries* in the 1860s and afterwards. They were almost exclusively concerned with medieval case law and ancient combats, and arguments about the last time trial by battle had been used to settle a dispute. Amongst all the column inches there was scarcely a mention of Mary.

She lived on in fiction, however, albeit far away from Warwickshire. Alice C. Benton contributed a short story titled *Trial by Combat* to a women's magazine published in Boston, Massachusetts. It was only tenuously anchored to the facts. Beautiful Mary Ashford and her gentle bookworm brother Philip move from London into a country cottage and are soon afterwards introduced to Abraham Thornton who clearly has Mary in his sights. She finds his crude manners and coarse speech repellent. Soon after Thornton learns that Mary's Welsh sweetheart Llewellyn Draper is due to return from a visit to his family, Mary is found dead, drowned in a stream. Thornton is tried and acquitted so Philip brings an appeal of murder against him, to which Thornton replies with a challenge to battle. Philip, being a slight young fellow, has to turn it down. Thornton soon afterwards flees to American where he dies of remorse. 'This event caused the right of appeal to be abolished by an act of parliament in 1819, it being the last case where a trial by combat could be called for,' writes Benton as if her fictional approximations were fact.

Fifty years after Mary died, even her grave became a target for revisionism. On 4 February 1867, the *Birmingham Daily Gazette* published a letter from a curmudgeonly local resident signing himself 'R.F.M.' Now that the railways had arrived in Sutton Coldfield, he moaned, Mary's grave had become even more popular with daytrippers up from the city who displayed 'the morbid curiosity of a certain class of holiday visitor'. One Saturday he saw sixty-four of these undesirables (he must have counted them) crowded round the slab making crude comments about the Reverend Luke Booker's inscription. It was time to get rid of the stone, he wrote. Mary had not been 'brutally violated' at all but had committed the sin of self-murder. The stone should be replaced with a plain one, giving just the facts. R.F.M. had already obtained permission from the Bishop of Worcester as well as, he claimed, the consent of Mary Ashford's relatives but the churchwardens were dragging their feet. He must have given up the fight because the gravestone remained in place.

By the middle of the century, the idea that Mary had not been raped and murdered became accepted by pretty much everyone, or at least those who were motivated to perpetuate the story in print. The veteran journalist Walter Thornbury, writing for Charles Dickens's magazine *All the Year Round* in 1867 — and published simultaneously in *Aris's Birmingham Gazette* — subscribed to it. The blood in the field was from 'natural causes', William Bedford and his friends were prejudiced against the accused, and if Mary was being attacked by Thornton she could have called out for help but didn't. For Thornbury, Mary was almost a simpleton. When she dressed for the party, she is 'in more than a girl's usual flutter of pretty vanity'. Before leaving her uncle's house, as she admires herself in the mirror, looking 'over her shoulder (after the manner of girls) to see that her shawl sets well, ruffles out her bonnet bows, and with little quick bird-like touches, arranges her glossy hair and set of her pink gown,' after which she runs singing down the lane. Thornbury could find no motive for Thornton killing Mary, but if he had, it would have been on her way up Bell Lane where she may have pressed him to promise marriage, and he in a rage might have thrown her into the pit. It was 'much more reasonable' to conjecture that the explanation lay with Mary herself. Either she was killed by a wandering tramp or she had gone down to the water to wash herself and had fallen in or she took the sudden decision to kill herself.

That Thornton was innocent was unquestioned. The alibi proved it. No wonder an anonymous journalist who reminisced about visiting William Ashford in Birmingham two years before he died felt he had to humour the old man in his absurd belief that Thornton was guilty. Ashford, he said, was 'quite warm' when speaking of Mary 'as though the affair had happened only a few weeks ago'. He could not sit still while talking about her but walked about the room gesticulating and occasionally moved to tears. It would have been cruel, says the writer, to suggest that she had not met her death at the hands of Thornton but had committed suicide 'at finding herself alone'.

In November 1924, Sir John Hall, 9th Baronet Dunglass, a retired army colonel who specialised in writing about historical mysteries, presented a monograph on the Mary Ashford case to an audience of worthy Edinburgh citizens. They were gripped by his strange tale of her killing, Thornton's acquittal, the appeal of murder and the dramatic throwing down of the gauntlet in the Court of King's Bench. Harry Hodge, who was always on the lookout for subjects for the *Notable British Trials* series he published with his brother William, wrote to Hall afterwards, suggesting he submit the story for a new volume. He was mindful of readers' sensibilities: 'Up till now, I have avoided anything of a sexual nature, as our readers are a varied class. In the case of Mary, however, there is nothing very obnoxious.'

Hall bought a collection of legal papers, including Sadler's brief for Thornton's defence, from William Bickley, a Birmingham local historian. *The Trial of Abraham Thornton*, which included an account of the trial and transcriptions of various original documents, was published in 1926. Sir John Hall's conclusion was that Thornton was a 'singularly unattractive figure' but was entirely innocent of the murder and that, having had sex early in the morning of 27 May, before she went to Mrs Butler's, Mary had died when she went down to the water's edge to wash herself, having carefully placed her belongings at the top of the pit, taking special care of her bonnet 'lest its yellow ribbons be splashed and suffer damage', slipped and drowned. He dismissed Omar Hall's statement as entirely self-serving.

Sir John Hall's was the last major historical examination of the case, although Mary Ashford's and Abraham Thornton's names, and themes associated with their stories, continued to crop up in academic works and dissertations on subjects such as women's history, popular theatre in the early nineteenth century and the literature of Walter Scott. In 2003, Patrick Hayes published a short semi-fictionalised account of the crime, and after weighing up the evidence for Thornton's guilt (half a page) and against (three pages) settled on the theory that the death had been an accidental killing during sexual intercourse: a date rape gone wrong. For Hayes, Thornton was an ordinary man, not the 'almost Frankenstein figure' created by the media, playwrights and Mary's defenders. 'He wasn't a vicious beast lurking in a dark alley... He was a young man with free will who had the capacity to do good or evil, like all of us.'

Chapter 14

'Too brutal to name'

The murder of Mary Ashford throws up a million questions. Who murdered her? Was it Abraham Thornton, the chief suspect? Or was it an untraceable vagrant? Was it even murder? Did Mary throw herself in the pit? Or did she fall in the water and drown? While the order of events before Mary died has been a mystery for centuries, there are other questions too. Why was Thornton acquitted despite strong circumstantial evidence? Was the trial botched, the judge biased, the jury bribed? And what part did misogyny play in the way Mary's behaviour was viewed? There was also an issue that resonates with the times we live in now; what part did the case play in shaping the national mood during a time of political and social turbulence?

When researching the death of Mary Ashford, my primary aim was to establish enough evidence to make a judgment on the likelihood of Thornton's guilt or innocence, although at the same time I had no special hope of coming up with a definitive answer. The issues thrown up by her death were interesting enough to justify looking at the whole episode again. It was clear that plenty of men at the time had a lot to say about the case, and only a few women since, and I wanted to use my femaleness to provide an alternative view.

A great deal of original material about the case has survived. Quite apart from the published trial reports, pamphlets, the many versions of the 'murder map', newspaper reports and broadsides, at Birmingham Archives there are boxes of correspondence, drafts of witness statements, stacks of legal documents and the brief for the defence written by Edward Sadler. My visit to see these resources was spent not in poring over them but in taking photographs to study later. At times, as I clicked away, I could not help but catch a fleeting sight of snippets of information and would scribble hasty notes: 'Look again at the list of Mary's clothes' or 'Why did Humpage say this?' When it came to John Bedford's original draft of Omar Hall's statement, taken on board the hospital ship, I did not pay too much attention. I had already seen the version Capper had sent to the Home Secretary, who had forwarded it on to William Bedford. I jotted it down in my notebook 'MS3069/13/72 — Hall's statement to John Bedford — transcribe.'

Weeks later, as I began to pull my knowledge about the case together, a narrative of what might have happened began to take shape although there were still many areas for which rational explanation eluded me. To help me think clearly, I plotted the events of 26 and 27 May 1817 on a spreadsheet, looking at them in terms of both the evidence and the psychology of the players. I had to be sure that I understood the motivation of every character at every stage.

Let's start with the party at Tyburn House, the first point we see Thornton in action. What do we know about his behaviour? He first saw Mary arrive with Hannah at the dance at around 8 o'clock and was immediately struck by her, quizzing his friend Joseph Cotterill on who she was (he later realised that he knew her from her days working at the Swan in Erdington). He declared he would 'have' her and boasted that he has previously 'had' her sister Ann three times. However, he appears not to have used the evening to flirt with her.

If Thornton wanted to seduce Mary why did he not make a move early, to give himself time to establish the beginnings of a relationship? After all, he expressed interest and at the end of the evening left the pub with her. It is likely that Thornton deliberately did not interact with Mary, as doing so would only provide her with an opportunity to reject him. Instead, he watched for the right moment. We can speculate that he had earlier seen Hannah come into the dancing room to tell Mary that she wanted to go home and knew that he would soon have to make his move.

Benjamin Carter saw Thornton dancing with Mary when he returned to the party because Hannah was growing impatient waiting for her friend on the bridge outside. Then, to the surprise of Hannah and Benjamin, Thornton joined them on the road home. How should we interpret this act of Thornton's? We should not assume that he was there at Mary's invitation or that she necessarily had any romantic interest in him, although she may have had. If Thornton chose to accompany them on their walk along the Chester Road, there would have been little she or the others could do to stop him. Even if Thornton had already proved to be a pest, Mary could reasonably assume that she would be safe, since she and her friends would be on the main road and she would be going to her grandfather's house at the crossroads. There was no great risk to her safety or reputation. On the other hand, Thornton's rapid and assertive insertion of himself into the group looks suspicious.

We know nothing of what Mary and Thornton talked about as they walked along. We have only Hannah and Benjamin's accounts about their progress down the road and their relative positions. To begin with, Mary and Thornton were in front. After Benjamin turned back to get something left at Tyburn House, Hannah walked on alone and eventually caught up with Mary and Thornton. She was alongside them for a short time, then overtook them, at which point Benjamin caught up first with Mary and Thornton and then with her. They must have been ambling along, in no great hurry. Did Thornton deliberately set the slow pace?

We can take a guess that it was probably about one o'clock when Hannah took a left-hand turn for Erdington, leaving Mary in the company of Thornton and Carter. She was not in the slightest bit perturbed at the prospect of walking alone down to her mother's house at Erdington Green, and no one else remarked on it, nor was she fearful of what might happen to Mary, otherwise she would not have left her. Women in the countryside were not generally afraid of attack and Thornton was, if not a personal acquaintance before that night, at least a part of the community and easily identifiable. It is more likely that Thornton offered polite assurances that he and Benjamin would accompany Mary to her grandfather's and that he would then walk back to Castle Bromwich. Benjamin went on ahead and left Mary with Thornton.

She was now alone with Thornton for the first time. Why did she not say goodnight to him and go in to her grandfather's? Did Thornton do something to prevent this, by detaining her in conversation, by flirting, kissing, embracing her, by *importuning* her for sex? Sex was, after all, his stated goal. He may have tried to coax her into the fields by reassuring her that he meant no harm, that it was just fun and that she had nothing to fear. Of course, it is entirely possible that she voluntarily reciprocated sexually to some extent. We have no way of knowing.

When I began this investigation, I was struck by the division between the male commentators who, by defending Mary's sexual honour, reduced her to a virginal sexless ideal, and those, in exonerating Thornton, played up the naturalness of her sexual feelings, albeit feelings that required a degree of coercion to be realised. However, even if Mary were in some degree attracted to Thornton, she also knew that they were not a courting couple. They had known each other for a matter of hours, perhaps only minutes, and had no history between their families (the allegation about Mary's sister Ann notwithstanding). Much would have been at stake in a decision to have sex with Thornton — loss of reputation, the risk of pregnancy, not to mention the ruin of her white dress. On balance, it seemed to me unlikely that Mary had consented to sex with Thornton at this stage of the night.

Thornton and Mary were alone together for two hours or more before the next, and last, positive sighting of them at the stile of the foredrove shortly after three o'clock. John Humpage's account of what he heard and saw is confused and confusing. He told the Coroner at Mary's inquest that at 3.15am, as he walked in Penns Mill Lane, he saw through the hedge what he thought was 'a woman in a light coloured dress' and heard a man talking loudly. He changed this evidence at the Warwick trial, when he said he was downstairs at Reynolds' cottage at about two o'clock and heard voices in the road, which continued until he left the house at 2.45am, and that he passed Mary and Thornton at the stile at 3am.

Both versions were a gift to Thornton's defence because they indicated that Mary had been in the fields with Thornton before she went down to Mrs Butler's and that she may have had sex with him there. As Justice Holroyd and many other commentators made clear, if Mary had sex with Thornton voluntarily Thornton had no need to stalk and rape her later. Thornton's solicitor Edward Sadler gave Humpage's evidence great weight in the brief for Thornton's defence team. He made a note next to his account of Humpage's testimony at the inquest: it 'shows clearly that the deceased and Prisoner had been in the field where the pit is, previous to witness passing them at the stile where he wished them Good Morning and therefore all those marks and appearances of persons having lain on the bank (which on the part of the prosecution are considered evidence of a rape) might have been made before Humpage passed them at the stile and wished them Good Morning.'

Thornton and Mary may have entered the fields early in the morning and kept to the footpath, not walking at all on the harrowed area, which meant that they left no trace of their movements. However, Humpage's evidence was so useful to Thornton's defence that it begs another question: why did he provide it? Was Humpage lying? In his statement, taken within hours of the crime, Thornton said he did not recognise Humpage (although he said Mary did – she thought she had seen him at the dance), but noticed that he had on a brown jacket; at the Warwick trial Humpage admitted that he knew Thornton. Given that it was three in the morning (albeit on a clear night and three days before a full moon), would Thornton really have been able to identify the shade of Humpage's coat? Or did he know and recognise Humpage? Could Thornton's father or perhaps Edward Sadler have paid

Humpage a visit before the inquest and asked him to give evidence with a particular slant or even to perjure himself?

At the inquest, Humpage said Mary tucked her dress behind her. He also said Mary and Thornton were 'leaning against the stile' so it is likely that the back of Mary's dress was not even visible to him. Humpage also stated, both at the inquest and at the trial, that Mary held her head down when he came by, which Sadler decided to interpret as resulting from shame at having recently had illicit sex.

A more likely scenario might be that during the hours he spent with Mary, Thornton had revealed himself as a sexual predator and social embarrassment. If Mary did hide her face from Humpage, could this have been because she did not want Humpage to spread rumours that she had been seen in Thornton's company? Mary was neither a naïve ninny nor the paragon conjured by the Reverend Luke Booker who was left fatally unable to protect herself for lack of a gallant or a matron. Mary would have known what to watch out for in men and how to protect herself. Twice a week she walked unaccompanied into Birmingham to sell produce from her uncle's farm at a regular pitch in the market. Here she stood amid the crowds — Birmingham folk in search of a bargain, fellow market traders and dealers, beggars, farmers, gangmasters, baker's and butcher's boys, messengers, thieves, pimps, prostitutes, ballad singers, pigs, cattle and horses — until her goods were gone or the day was over. The crude language she would have heard and the behaviour she witnessed would have taught her to fend off pilferers and con artists as well as chancers offering coarse sexual invitations. If her family did not think she could cope with this and emerge with her reputation unscathed, they would not have sent her. We can feel confident that Mary would have recognised Thornton's swaggering and boasts for what they were. We may also wonder whether at this point in the night she realised that the man with her had been involved with her sister Ann and whether Ann had warned her about him.

Why did Mary not make her excuses to Thornton and head back down to her grandfather's? It was only a five-minute walk. One explanation might be that at this point, or shortly before, she realised that she was bleeding. (It is unlikely that she told Thornton about this. Apart from the fact that there were deep taboos about periods, there was no reason to.) She was wearing a white gown, white spencer and white stockings. They were finer and more expensive than her working clothes. She may have been a low-paid servant but she cared enough about her appearance to plan her look and coordinate her clothes carefully. Moreover, the white dress may not even have belonged to her but to a friend or a sister. If she had started her period, she would have wanted to change into her working dress as soon as possible and she had no alternative but to go to Mrs Butler's to do that.

She and Thornton walked past the crossroads and headed towards Erdington, during which time Mary would have been looking out for an opportunity to shake off this troublesome man. One soon presented itself. After promising to wait for Thornton while he went to relieve himself in a field near the horsepit on Bell Lane, Mary sped on ahead. This was when Thomas Asprey, who was near Greensall's farm, saw her as he headed northwards. The road was straight and wide here and he could see for over 400 yards (366m) along it. He looked down the lane and saw no one but Mary Ashford. He noticed that she was walking 'very fast' but did not see Thornton.

As for Thornton, his plan had gone awry. He had fully expected Mary to wait for him while he was relieving himself but instead she had insulted and humiliated him by rushing off without a word. She had not capitulated in the fields (if she was ever there) so he needed to adjust his sights. He knew she would be taking the shortcut to Penns Mill Lane on her way back so he would lurk in a field there and then 'have' her.

For the time being, we will leave Thornton near the horsepit and follow Mary as she reached Mrs Butler's house. After Hannah let her in, Mary changed her clothes, taking off her white frock, spencer and stockings. These items, along with the half-boots, were later found in the bundle by the pit. The white stockings were bloodstained, the dress less so. Thornton's supporters, assuming the blood on the stockings to be from her broken hymen, said that this proved Mary had had sex before she changed her clothes, conveniently forgetting that a more reasonable explanation was that the blood was menstrual. Mary may have bled a little into the dress while leaning against or sitting on the stile; according to John Bird, the factory manager at Penns, there were a few spots on the back of the dress presented at the inquest.

Menstrual blood does not always flow evenly, especially at the beginning. If the flow was light, she may have felt that it was not worth asking Hannah for rags and that an easier solution to the issue of 'feminine hygiene' was to take off the white stockings, which she gartered under the knee and were probably already a little dirty from dancing, and, while Hannah was out of the room, give herself a discreet wipe. It would do for now.

After Mary emerged from Mrs Butler's house and headed north up Bell Lane she was seen by Joseph Dawson, John Kesterton and Thomas

Broadhurst. None of them saw Thornton. She passed her grandfather's house at the crossroads and continued along Bell Lane, turning into the foredrove, going over the stile and up the footpath towards Penns Lane. Here, probably at the south-west corner of the harrowed field, she was confronted by Thornton.

How can we be confident that Thornton was in the harrowed field and not on his way to Holden's via Erdington Green? First, a number of people had stories about 'confessions' made by Thornton, from the vague statement he made to John Hackney, who arrested him on the writ of appeal, that he 'believed if he had not gone with her it [the murder] would not have happened' to his more specific admission to Mr Davis, the stonemason, while in Birmingham Gaol 'that the girl died under him, and being dead he threw her into the pit.'

Omar Hall's statement about the rape and the visits Thomas Dales made to Thornton was much more detailed. It started with a claim that Thornton had admitted raping and killing Mary. How reliable a witness was Hall? He certainly had a track record of slipperiness, fraud and deception. Those who had had direct dealings with him, Thomas Capper, the Superintendent of Hulks, and the captain of the *Justitia*, were sceptical of his statement and advised the Bedfords not to give it credence. Hall also had an incentive for making his revelations. He was to be sent to New South Wales imminently, and to appear in court would require the Home Secretary to grant him an unconditional pardon. However, just because Hall had a motive to lie does not mean that he was lying.

The statement Capper took down on 2 November included scant details of the rape:

> '[Thornton] confessed to have committed the rape, and said in what way it was done, which is too brutish to name. In regard to the murder he never fully confessed to putting her into the pit in a living state, although in all his transactions and conversations signified to me that he done done so in a dead one.'

Information about the rape that Omar Hall gave to John Bedford *in person*, while on the *Alonzo* hospital ship, was quite different. In the Birmingham Archives there are two versions of his statement, the first with words scratched out, inserted and overwritten, is practically illegible. A second, cleaner version was made afterwards. Neither of them have been quoted in previous studies of the case. Why was this? Did earlier researchers decipher the documents and then take a decision to ignore them? My guess is that the reason lies in the combination of the illegible scrawl, the awful, dismaying language Omar Hall used (the description of the rape would not be suitable for ladies — Sir John Hall's 1926 study of the case just scraped through on that measure) and Hall's reputation as a liar.

What did Hall allege that Thornton said, that could not be repeated in public?

'Thornton told this Examinant [Hall] that he had had connection with the girl (meaning Mary Ashford), that it happened upon the grass, that he had not a fair strike at her, that she shuffled her arse about in such a way that he could scarcely get into her. That he spent himself before he got into her. He had a good deal of trouble to manage her and that she was not so quick a piece as her sister. That she fainted under him, but that he said that it was an old trick of women and he had had them so before and that he fetched some water and sprinkled it in her face but that she was then in a dead state. And that the doctor had perjured himself for that she was not in a living state when he tossed her into the pit.'

As I read and transcribed this passage, so different from the cleaned-up version sent by Capper to the Home Secretary, I knew immediately that Hall was quoting Thornton's real voice. The words are so powerful that it is difficult to think them anything other than authentic. The style of language used was an abrupt change from the preceding sentences, which were standard legalese for statements. John Bedford asked questions of Hall and carefully wrote down his words: '...That Thornton knew this Examinant's former situation in life, courted the acquaintance of this Examinant, and...frequently advised him as to his (Thornton's) case, and at times opened his mind very freely to this Examinant on the subject, viz that after they had been together about five days or a week, Thornton told this Examinant...' and so on. By contrast, the confession was almost breathless: 'Happened upon the grass... not a fair strike at her... she shuffled her arse about... he could scarcely get into her... spent himself before he got into her... trouble to manage her... not so quick a piece as her sister... an old trick of women...' The deletions and insertions on the draft version were perhaps signs that Bedford could not quite keep up with what Hall was saying.

Can I prove that this was the 'smoking gun'? No. There will always be a suspicion that Omar Hall was manipulative enough to make it up. This was reported speech, given in an account written months after the conversation with Thornton took place. Nevertheless, this section of Hall's statement has freshness and immediacy. It was intimate talk between men — misogynist, hubristic, boastful. Thornton sounded like he was on a roll, eager to convey the excitement of the moment, the remembrance made all the more thrilling because he was sure he would get away with it. This was not so much a confession as a rhapsody.

Omar Hall's statement also contains a clue to the mystery of the single footmark on the bank of the pit:

'That he applied the print which he said could not be seen of his foot on the turf to the turf at the edge of the pit.'

Thornton had deliberately created a train of footprints in order to fool investigators into thinking Mary had walked to the pit before throwing herself in. These had simply been missed by Lavell, Bird and Webster. Edward Holroyd, who supported the idea that Mary's death was a tragic accident, had theorised that Mary's footprints had evaporated with the dew, but in reality it was Thornton's fake evidence that had done so.

In his written statement made during the examination by William Bedford, Thornton said that he went down to Erdington Green to see if he could see Mary and waited five minutes for her. According to verbal statements made to his solicitor, he and Mary had already had sex in the field, so why would he do this? Was he looking for more sex? Or was it to arrange another rendezvous? And if either of these, or for any other reason, why did he stay only five minutes?

He also claimed that once he decided to give up the wait he walked along a series of footpaths and roads to the south of the village, crossed the Birmingham and Fazeley canal and came to Holden's farm. This is what Thornton says about the encounter: he 'went by Shipley's in his road home and afterwards by John Holden's where he saw a man and woman with some milk cans and a young man driving some cows out of a field who he thought to be Holden's son.' He did not claim that anyone else saw him, nor did he claim that he knew the Jennens. It was easy enough to identify them. On Wednesday, the day after Thornton's arrest, William Bedford or Edward Sadler must have asked John Holden who they were, and contacted them on Thursday or Friday to instruct them to attend Mary's inquest.

Their evidence of the time they saw Thornton was the basis of his alibi yet neither of them had a pocket watch and they were not within hearing of a church clock. At the trial William Jennens described his convoluted formula for calculating the time:

'Before [Martha Jennens asked Jane Heaton, Holden's servant, the time], and after I saw the Prisoner, we had milked a cow a piece, in the yard, which might occupy us about ten minutes. The cows were not in the yard then, they were a field's breadth from the house.'

Jennens used a different formula at the inquest:

'I had four cows to milk and four people to milk them so they were fifteen to twenty minutes milking. When they finished I asked Holden's servant what time it was — she said seventeen minutes to five.'

At the Warwick trial, William and Martha Jennens insisted that Thornton was walking slowly as he came past the farm; subsequently, when the Bedfords were trying to build the second case against Thornton, two separate witnesses said that William Jennens himself had contradicted this after the Warwick trial. He told them that Thornton was actually 'in great haste' and moving 'at a great pace'. Why would Jennens backtrack? Common sense tells us that if he had lied under oath in court, he would keep quiet about it. One interpretation is that Jennens was unable to bear the burden of keeping this secret and felt compelled to divest himself of it by telling the truth. The knowledge that his evidence had led to a grievous miscarriage of justice set him apart from his neighbours and friends, most of whom were disgusted and outraged by the verdict, and destroying his own credibility was a way to once more be included in the fold. Alcohol also had a part to play. Jennens was drinking in the pub when he had these conversations.

When Thornton was next seen, at about five o'clock at the floodgates near Zachariah Twamley's mill, it was by his friend John Heydon, who was taking up nets. They talked for fifteen minutes during which Thornton said he had taken 'a wench' home. This was not true, even according to his own sworn statement, but was probably accepted as harmless male exaggeration. The next sighting, by John Woodcock, Zachariah Twamley's miller, was at ten past five. Woodcock heard Mr Rotton's stable clock strike five, went into a wheat field and when he emerged saw the two men talking by the floodgates, calculating the time by retracing his movements afterwards.

All of the evidence of Jennens, Heydon and Woodcock at the Warwick trial relied on estimated times and was not effectively challenged by the prosecution team. Justice Holroyd did not point up any of the weaknesses in the alibi, simply telling the jury that for Thornton to have committed the murder he would have had a maximum of twenty minutes to do it and get to Holden's. Holroyd gave the jury a firm instruction only to convict if they were fully satisfied of Thornton's guilt so it is not surprising that Thornton was acquitted. His alibi had been presented as incontrovertible. In October, after Thornton had been rearrested, John Tibbits who had sat on the jury, told John Bedford that his own opinion was that Thornton was guilty but they could not find him so on the evidence, and that the timings were 'the only thing that turned their verdict in favour of the prisoner.'

John Hiscox, the London attorney who became obsessed with disproving the alibi, dismissed the evidence of all the defence witnesses as mere guesswork or tainted by friendship (John Heydon), and focused instead on James White who saw Thornton half a mile from Shard End at 5.10am, Hiscox's calculation of the true time. Thomas Broadhurst saw Mary at 4.03 half a mile from the pit and walking fast. She would have reached it at 4.10. That would have given Thornton an hour to rape and murder her and run or walk the 3.5 miles to Shard End by way of Holden's farm and Twamley's mill. Hiscox thought Thornton had run for about half the distance. By my calculation, with Thornton travelling for 15 minutes at a slow running pace (7mph) and for 26 minutes at an average walking pace (4mph), he would have had 19 minutes to rape Mary, throw her in the pit and arrange her belongings on the bank. If, on the other hand, Thornton had done as he said he had, parted from Mary at the horsepit at 3.15, and gone home via Erdington and along the footpath to Holden's and then to Castle Bromwich, where he was seen by James White at 5.10, he would have had almost two hours to travel 2.9 miles (4.8km), an average walking speed of only 1.5mph, which begs the question, why was he walking slowly? And why was he not seen at any point before he reached Holden's farm?

Thornton's supporters pointed to his unasked-for disclosures of information relevant to the case as a sign of his innocence. These otherwise intelligent men forgot that these statements were of facts that would have been known or found out very quickly in any event. 'Why I was with her until four in the morning!' was not of any particular help to investigators. They knew he had been with her in the night. It is possible that at the time he said this to Daniel Clarke, he misjudged the time Mary left him at the horsepit (there is no evidence he carried his own watch). He also offered information that he had had sex with Mary (whether it was before or after Dales examined his clothes is not really as important as William Bedford thought it was). Again, he would have difficulty explaining the blood on his clothes any other way. That he did not change out of them once he reached home was not a sign of innocence but of its diametrical opposite — a cynical attempt to look innocent by appearing to be unaware that he was incriminating himself.

Rape is not sex and it is not about sex. It is about anger, control and violence. Not all rapes and not all rapists are alike. Today, Thornton's attack on Mary Ashford might be classed by investigators as an acquaintance rape as she and Thornton had known each other a short time and she was, during the early hours of 27 May at least, in his company voluntarily.

Doctors Ronald and Stephen Holmes, who have pioneered the sociopsychological profiling of rapists by studying over 600 murders and rapes, have developed a tool now widely used by US police agencies. They divided rapists into four types, each with quite different motivations: the Power Reassurance rapist, who is prone to self-doubt and attacks women in order to enhance his self-confidence; the Anger Retaliation rapist, who expresses his rage towards women and wants to punish and degrade them, sometimes choosing a victim at random; the Anger Excitation rapist, who gains sexual gratification from controlling, hurting or torturing his victim; and the Power Assertive rapist, who sees rape as a confirmation of his virility.

The Power Assertive rapist has an extreme sense of superiority and entitlement; he is domineering in the home, believes men are superior to women and takes pride in his masculinity. On the surface, he appears to have no self-doubt although deep down he may be insecure about women. For him, rape is merely something that men do — it is not a crime and he feels no guilt over it. Women are sex objects but the rape is not for sex, it is for power and predation, to humiliate the victim. His mode of attack is to use 'confidence' to gain the trust of his victim, by appearing to be reliable and gentlemanly, by offering to walk a woman home, for instance, during which he will seek to put her out of reach of help.

The typical Power Assertive rapist also cares a great deal about his appearance; he is athletic, exercises often and dresses flashily. He tends to be loud and boisterous and to work in a male-dominated field, such as construction or the military, and will behave in a hyper-macho way. He likes

126

to impress other men. In his leisure time, he socialises in places where he has plenty of females to select a victim from and where alcohol is available: he will try to incapacitate his victim by getting her drunk. He generally attacks away from where he lives and chooses a victim within his own age group.

As for the attack itself, this is usually opportunistic rather than the result of a long thought-out plan. He generally has the strength to force his victim without using a weapon, but he might bring one with him, and he is happy to use a moderate level of force (he will readily use his fists). Resistance and pleading will enrage him and increase the violence. To intimidate, he will slap, hit, swear and rip clothes. Often, he will not be able to reach ejaculation and will force his victim to perform oral sex to keep the rape going. He is very brutal and he might kill but that is not usually his intention.

No rapist ticks all the boxes, but from the evidence, Abraham Thornton appears to fit the profile of a Power Assertive rapist. A burly bricklayer (and sometime mower of barley fields), fit enough to cross country at speed without appearing to break sweat (the murder was committed before he grew fat in Warwick Gaol), who dressed carefully (his smart black coat and hat and yellow waistcoat spring to mind), who boasted to his male friends about 'having' Ann Ashford and thought nothing of announcing his intention to have Mary too, who opportunistically and rapidly inserted himself into the party walking home on the Chester Road, offered to see Mary home and then prevented her from going to her grandfather's house.

Thornton would have seen Mary's rapid escape, while he was relieving himself in the field, as disrespecting his masculinity and it would have angered him. In his statement to Bedford, Thornton coolly stated, 'Mary Ashford walked on and Examinant never saw her afterwards.' Ten days after their interview on the *Alonzo*, Omar Hall wrote to John Bedford with some further revelations:

> 'Thornton said, Mary, walk·on and I will overtake you. He got over a gate to ease himself and when he returned into the lane she was gone out of sight... Had she waited so as he could have seen her again, then he should have parted with her and had no desire to have seen her afterwards and then nothing would have happened.'

These were probably disingenuous lies because Thornton was looking for his first chance to rape Mary but here he was merely doing what many rapists do; blaming the victim for her own misfortune.

The frenzied footmarks in the harrowed field were evidence that Mary, once confronted, did not comply, that she had desperately tried to evade him. Thornton may have been trying to use 'confidence' as well as threats to subdue Mary, and this may have been the point at which Mary, hoping to disgust Thornton, pleaded that she was 'not fit'; Thornton would have replied that he did not care about that. According to the Holmeses, begging and crying are rarely effective with Power Assertive rapists; it just enrages them.

In a letter to the Quaker banker Paul Moon James, John Bird theorised that because the footmarks showed that Thornton was on Mary's right side in the field, it was likely that he administered a blow to that side of her head before they were on the ground. Bird wrote that, according to the witnesses who saw her body when it was retrieved from the pit:

> '…She most certainly had received a blow or blows to the head on the right side of the face and neck, the right nostril bled very freely when taken out and after the body was cleaned and laid out a small quantity of bloody liquid ran out of the right eye and down the cheek, evidence sufficient I think to prove a contusion, though not by any of the witnesses thought sufficient to have caused her death.'

Calling out for help while being attacked was, as we have seen, an important part of proving a rape, so the absence of Mary's screams was understood, by some at least, to mean that there was no rape. Humpage was questioned at Warwick about the distance from Reynolds' cottage, where he was courting Martha Reynolds, to the pit, which he underestimated at a hundred yards, the implication being that if Mary had screamed while he was in the house or in the Lane, he would have heard it. Actually, William Lavell, who lived next door to the Reynolds house, said it was 'between two and three hundred yards' — but it made no difference anyway. At no point in the trial or at the inquest did anyone come forward to say that they had heard screaming coming from the field or the pit.

However, in Birmingham Archives there is a second-hand report that screams were heard. According to John Bird, 'a man who lives near Erdington heard two screams at an interval of about a minute from each other on the 27 May at about 20 minutes past 4. He could hear no more screams, though he listened some little time longer and then not expecting anything particular, resumed his work.'

Bird was sure that Thornton was guilty but was at first puzzled by some logistical aspects of the case. For instance, why had Thornton raped Mary so close to Penns Mill Lane, virtually on the public footpath? Surely, he would have feared discovery. After all, the shortcut was a well-worn route. George Jackson, for one, used it every day. Bird's theory was that Thornton knew that the people in Reynolds's cottage had been awake less than an hour and a half before he attacked Mary and he used this to give false reassurance to her. After the 'running and dodging' in the harrowed field he may have subdued Mary enough to persuade her to come with him towards the stile in the top corner of the field and through to the footpath beyond. 'Would she not think that by going nearer to the houses she would be safe?' wrote Bird.

As for Thornton, he had a specific reason for committing the crime in such an open space. 'It would now, in going down the hedge side, be your policy to reconnoitre the country to observe if anyone was in the lane or at the houses,' continued Bird, putting himself in Thornton's shoes, 'but this you cannot do until you arrive at the precise spot where the rape was committed. From that spot, you command a perfect view of the front of the houses, and down the lane beyond them, also up the lane higher than the top of the barley field.'

According to Omar Hall, once Thornton had hit Mary or subdued her enough not to resist, and had got her on the ground under the tree, she 'shuffled her arse' so much he did not get 'a fair strike' at her and became even more angry. Perhaps it was during this struggle that Thornton hit Mary again and she became unconscious. It is interesting that, according to Hall's statement at least, Thornton 'spent himself before he got into her' — another characteristic typical of Power Assertive rapists.

We should not assume that at the beginning of the attack it was Thornton's intention to kill Mary but he certainly meant her harm and his attack was violent. He may well have been surprised that he had knocked her out and went down to the pit for water in a panicked attempt to revive her. Omar Hall's statement has him asserting that pretending to be unconscious is a trick 'many' women pull, which would suggest that Thornton had been in this situation before. Feigning unconsciousness to mitigate beatings is a known tactic used by rape victims. Thornton's observation that Mary 'was not so quick a piece as her sister' also points to him being a serial rapist. We can surmise that the reason Ann Ashford survived was that she was easier to overcome.

Once Thornton realised that Mary would not wake up, he had to think quickly and immediately came up with a plan to make her death look like suicide. The first thing he did was to position her belongings carefully on the bank. Omar Hall's letter to John Bedford explained it: 'Anyone might plainly see the clothes on the bank as they passed and would suppose she had made away with herself.' This message convinced a considerable number of people.

Fuelled by adrenaline, Thornton showed great presence of mind. He knew that he would have to get as far away from the pit as quickly as possible and that he would need an alibi. First he retraced his steps across the top of the field towards the dry pit, possibly to retrieve something (we can speculate that it was a dropped handkerchief, which was said to be missing from Mary's body or perhaps it was a shoe). Or he may have intended to head down through Erdington village, where he was sure to be seen, but then thought better of it. Erdington was not sufficiently far away to put him out of the frame. He must have remembered that the milk people come to Holden's farm early in the morning and instead went across trespass land, through barley fields, and over hedges and stiles.

There is no doubt in my mind that Abraham Thornton was guilty of the rape and murder of Mary Ashford. His alibi, based on estimated timings by people who did not carry their own watches or who referred to clocks that were wrong, was shaky, and there remains a strong but unproven suspicion that at least some of the witnesses, Thomas Dales among them, were bribed. Thornton's numerous divulgences to other men about his encounter with Mary speak of someone who was so eager to impress, to take part in macho posturing, that he could not stop himself broadcasting his 'conquest'. Each and every time, he blamed his victim for the rape.

People who have been raped sometimes compare the experience of giving evidence in court to another brutal assault. It was no different in 1817. Victims, even dead ones, were subjected to the same aggressive scepticism; defend the accused by denigrating the victim. One of the more tragic aspects of this case is that while Mary attracted a great many supporters, for the first few years after her death at least, we cannot but wonder whether this would be true had she survived her encounter with Thornton or had some previous stain on her reputation.

Edward Sadler may have bent the evidence to fit his client's alibi because he sincerely believed that Thornton was innocent. He was not alone in making assumptions about Mary that arose from deep prejudice against women and even deeper prejudice against women who had been raped. In the minds of many, rape was almost impossible, and women's capitulation in the face of 'importunity' was only proof that they consented. A good rape victim, one who did not consent, was almost always a dead one, because to survive would be to suffer a 'fate worse than death'.

The prosecution of Thornton was botched by William Bedford and the barristers, who did not adequately address the weaknesses of the alibi. It was also hampered by unclear medical evidence. Although the surgeons who examined Mary were certainly hamstrung by their lack of experience and knowledge they showed little initiative; they offered no explanation for the two deep and fresh lacerations to Mary's 'parts of generation', which surely could not arise from consensual sex, and leaves us grimly wondering what Thornton did to create them. They appear not to have looked for injuries to Mary's head or to have noted the bruises on her upper arms.

Of all the contemporary commentators on the case, John Hiscox was the only one who managed to combine an analysis of the defects in Thornton's alibi with an understanding of human behaviour – he knew that it took more than one instance of illicit sex to cause a normally healthy, happy young woman suddenly to drown herself. He was absolutely certain Thornton was guilty, as were the men and women of Erdington and Penns Mill who had seen the footmarks in the harrowed field, the 'lake of blood' and Mary's battered body as it was taken out of the water.

This was a story of missed chances and misunderstandings. If William Bedford and the prosecution barristers had thought more forensically about what Mary did and where she was in the early hours of 27 May, if they had paid more attention to Thornton's alibi, if they had given more credence to Omar Hall's vivid and shocking statement, if they had pressed the Home Secretary more forcefully to grant Hall a pardon, it is possible that the appeal of murder would have been allowed without a trial by battle and Thornton would have been found guilty of the heinous crime he surely committed.

Instead, he headed off to America, leaving a trail of rumour and supposition in his wake. Who knows what he did there. Unfortunately, we can be fairly sure that he would have found new victims to bully and terrify. As for Mary, whose reputation, freedoms, independence, sexuality and intelligence were so fiercely disputed, I can only hope that this investigation into her murder corrects some of the erroneous assertions that have been made about her and puts right, in some small degree, a missed opportunity for justice.

Voluntary Examination of Abraham Thornton

Author's note: There were some small but significant differences between the version of Thornton's statement quoted in trial reports and that copied by his attorney Edward Sadler into his brief for the defence barristers (the version given here, which is taken from MS3078/1/8 Folio 33–4 in Birmingham Archives), the most important of which was that most of the printed versions included the sentence 'Examinant further said, that when he got home, it wanted twenty minutes to five, by his father's clock,' while Sadler's version did not. It is impossible to know whether this inaccuracy crept in from a mishearing or whether it was something the defence asserted outside court.

27 May 1817

Who said he was a bricklayer, that he came to the Three Tuns at Tyburn about 6 o'clock last night where there was a dance, that he danced a dance or two with the landlord's daughter but whether he danced with Mary Ashford not he cannot recollect. Examinant stayed till about 12 o'clock. He then went with Mary Ashford, Benjamin Carter and a young woman who he understood to be Mr Machin's housekeeper of Erdington, that they walked together as far as Mr Potter's, Carter and the housekeeper went on towards Erdington. Examinant and Mary Ashford went on as far as Mr Freeman's. They then turned to the right and went along a lane till they came to a gate and stile on the right hand side of the road. They went over the stile and into the next piece and along the footroad. They continued along the footroad 4 or 5 fields but cannot exactly tell how many. Examinant and Mary Ashford then returned the same road when they came to the gate and stile they first got over. They stood there about 10 minutes or 1/4 of an hour talking. It might be then about 3 o'clock and whilst they stood there a man came by. Examinant did not know who. Had on a jacket of a brown colour, the man was coming along the footpath they had returned along. Examinant said Good Morning and the man said the same. Examinant asked Mary Ashford if she knew the man. She said she did not know whether she knew him or not but thought he was one who had been at Tyburn. That examinant and Mary Ashford stayed at the stile 1/4 of an hour afterwards. They then went straight up to Freeman's again. Crossed the road and went on towards Erdington. Mary Ashford walked on and Examinant never saw her afterwards. She was nearly opposite Mr Greensall's. Whilst he was in the field he saw a man cross the road for James's but did not know who he was. He then went on for Erdington workhouse to see if he could see Mary Ashford. He stopped upon the green about five minutes to wait for her. It was then 4 o'clock or 10 minutes past 4 o'clock. Examinant went by Shipley's in his road home and afterwards by John Holden's where he saw a man and woman with some milk cans and a young man driving some cows out of a field who he thought to be Holden's son. He then went towards Mr Twamley's mill where he saw Mr Rotton's keeper taking rubbish out the nets at the floodgates. He asked the man what o'clock it was. He answered near 5 o'clock or 5. He knew the keeper. Twamley's mill is about a mile and a quarter from his father's house with whom he lives. The first person he saw was Edward Leek, a servant of his father's and a boy. That his mother was up. He took off a black coat he had on and put on the one he now wears which hung up in the kitchen and changed his hat and left them both in the house. He did not change his shoes or his stockings though his shoes were rather wet from having walked across the meadows. That Examinant knew Mary Ashford when she lived at The Swan at Erdington, but not particularly intimate with her. That he had not seen the said Mary Ashford for a considerable time before he met her at Tyburn. Examinant had been drinking the whole evening, but not so much as to be intoxicated.

Omar Hall's Statement to John Y. Bedford

Author's note: This is the version I deciphered from John Bedford's draft, apparently taken down verbatim on the hospital ship *Alonzo* and is transcribed from MS3069/13/3/72 in Birmingham Archives.

7 November 1817

Omar Hall states that he was confined with Thornton and slept in the same cell at Warwick Gaol about six weeks. That in about 5 days after they had been together in their confinement together Thornton told him the particulars of the connection he had with the girl, that it happened upon the grass, that he had not a fair stroke at her, that she shuffled her arse about in such a way that he could scarcely get into her. That he spent himself before he got into her. That he had a good deal [of trouble] to manage her. That she was not so quick a piece as her sister. That she fainted under him, but that he said that it was an old trick of women and he had had them so before and that he fetched some water and sprinkled it in her face but that she was then in a dead state. And that the doctor had perjured himself for that she was not in a living state when he tossed her into the pit. That he applied the print which he said could not be seen of his foot on the turf to the turf at the edge of the pit. That he told examinant the conversation between himself and Dale respecting the handkerchief, the blood upon his shirt and have happened when Dale first took him into custody.

That about a week after Thornton mentioned to examinant the time when he had first conversation with Dale they were walking together in the courtyard a person (whom Thornton told examinant was Dale) called Thornton to him at the turnkey's kitchen window. He went to him and they remained in conversation together about 5 or 7 minutes. Saw Thornton with the letter to Dale as well as direct it. It was very small. The letter

134

was directed to Mr Thomas Dale Birmingham. The reason he ascribed for writing this letter was that he wanted to say something more to Dale as the turnkey came while he was talking to him at the turnkey's window which prevented his saying all he wanted to then. That Dale had a good deal eased his mind but he wanted to know whether his father had fully settled it with him. There was something else he wanted to say to Dale which he did not name to examinant. This he believes was the substance of the letter to Dale but he did not see the contents of it. Examinant offered to write the letter for him to read on the sly but he said it would not do for it must be in his own handwriting. Examinant told Thornton that he had better consult with his lawyer about the shoe marks and other things how far he thought him guilty. Thornton said that his lawyer and his family were on very friendly terms and that he did not wish him to know more about the matter than he was acquainted with already. His lawyer said to him when he was before the magistrate alluding to his deposition 'You had better not sign it' Thornton said there was nothing in it but the truth and then the lawyer said "Why then Abraham thee had better sign it" which he said he did sign and therefore it was that he did not like to alter what he had before stated to his attorney or to ask him his opinion about it.

Omar Hall came to this ship the 17th September last, the first time he mentioned the subject of this case was about a week afterwards to Hill and Haynes who came on board with him. He came on board the *Justitia* on the 23rd of July from which he was moved to this ship. Saw one paper about Thornton's trial while on board the *Justitia* and two since he has been on board this ship – he never saw any particular account of the trial.

Illustrations

Cameo of Mary Ashford, from Cooper, J. (1818). *A Report of the Proceedings Against Abraham Thornton at Warwick Summer Assizes, 1817, for the Murder of Mary Ashford; and, subsequently, In the Court of King's Bench, in an Appeal of the Said Murder.* Warwick: Heathcote and Foden (author's collection).

Portrait of Abraham Thornton published in the *Observer*, 8 February 1818 (author's collection).

Cottages in Erdington, Warwickshire (author's photograph).

Tyburn House and Shard End, reproduced with kind permission of the Library of Birmingham (Benjamin Stone Collection, Box 2, Print 38 and Box 28, Print 24).

'Birmingham in England.' *The New York Public Library Digital Collections.* 'The Miriam and Ira D. Wallach Division of Art, Prints and Photographs: Print Collection, The New York Public Library.

Map and details of harrowed field and cross-section of pit by Rowland Hill, included in Cooper, J., (author's collection).

'Penns Lane, adjoining the scene of Mary Ashford's death', based on an engraving by Samuel Lines, from Dent, R.K. (1880), *Old and New Birmingham.* Birmingham: Houghton and Hammond.

'The Murder Pit', photograph reproduced with kind permission of the Library of Birmingham (WK/E2/497).

Portable kit for an autopsy, made in London by S. Maw & Son (1860), reproduced with kind permission of Science Museum, London, Wellcome Images.

ILLUSTRATIONS

Mary Ashford's grave in Sutton Coldfield churchyard, reproduced with kind permission of the Library of Birmingham (WK/S17/23).

New Street, Birmingham, from Hutton, W. (1809). *A History of Birmingham.* Birmingham: Knott & Lloyd.

Reverend Luke Booker, Vicar of Dudley, by William J. Pringle. Reproduced with kind permission of Dudley Council Museum Service.

Warwick Shire Hall, copyright Paul Harrop, with kind permission (www.geograph.org.uk/photo/4483705).

Exterior of Westminster Hall (1798), by Samuel Ireland, reproduced with kind permission of Yale Center for British Art, Paul Mellon Collection.

Abraham Thornton by William Thomas Fry, reproduced with kind permission of Science Museum, London, Wellcome Images.

'Diligence and Dissipation' (1797), print by Thomas Gaugain and Thomas Hellyer, after James Northcote (1746-1831). Courtesy of Yale Center for British Art, Paul Mellon Fund.

Jeremiah Brandreth, from *the Observer*, 26 October 1818 (author's collection).

Mary Ashford, engraved by J. Thompson from a portrait by John Partridge (author's collection).

Hulks at Plymouth (undated) by Samuel Prout, reproduced with kind permission of Yale Center for British Art, Paul Mellon Collection.

Gauntlet, fellow to that thrown down in Westminster Hall, reproduced with kind permission of the Library of Birmingham (WK/MISC/5).

'Trial by Combat' from Myers, P.V.N. (1917). *A History of Rome.* Boston: Ginn and Co.

Mr C. Kemble as Ivanhoe. Courtesy of Billy Rose Theatre Division, The New York Public Library.

'The dance of death: the duel' (1816) by Thomas Rowlandson, reproduced with kind permission of Science Museum, London, Wellcome Images.

'The last scene of *Trial by Battle*' from Wilkinson, R. (1819). *Londina Illustrata*. Vol. 2. London: Robert Wilkinson. Courtesy of Tufts University Digital Collections & Archives.

Royal Coburg Theatre in 1820 (author's collection).

Acknowledgements

This book would not have been possible with the help and advice given by my esteemed agent Hedda Archbold of HLA Agency and the support of my long-suffering partner Tim Clifford. Thank you also to all the friends and relations who have encouraged me. You know who you are, but Barbara Segall, Karen Robinson, Jane Cook, Alison McIndoe, Adam Roberts, Louise Lyon and Nick Jones deserve special mention. The staff at Birmingham Archives, Erdington Library and the British Library were unfailingly helpful, as were the team at Pen & Sword: Katie Eaton, Lauren Burton, Laura Hirst, Tara Moran and Carol Trow. Finally, a shout-out to Roger N. Wright, Professor Emeritus at Rensselaer Polytechnic Institute in Troy, New York, who explained to me the importance of marl in the wire-drawing industry. Needless to say, all mistakes are mine. I apologise for them in advance.

Sources

The repercussions from the death of Mary Ashford were many. The impact of the two legal processes that resulted left not only emotional ripples but legal ones too. As one might expect with a case of this magnitude, there is a mountain of primary and secondary source material: many different versions of the first trial at Warwick, numerous pamphlets about the guilt or otherwise of Abraham Thornton, followed by tract upon tract detailing the history of and legal precedents for trial by battle. In addition, there are the documents preserved by the lawyers involved, reams of newspaper reports and the occasional reminiscence of the case. Where accounts differed, I have tried to establish the facts using 'best guess'. Below, I have listed the primary sources, many of which are in the Birmingham Archive.

Original text is quoted accurately but occasionally I have amended or regularised spelling, punctuation and capitalisation in order to aid understanding. There is a variety of spellings for the names of witnesses. Thomas Asprey, for example, is also given as Astpree and Aspree; Humpage is also Hompidge and Umpage. Generally I have used the versions I have found in birth, marriage and death records.

Birmingham Archives
MS1021, MS3078/1/8, MS3069/13/3/72, MAP 304097, MS477/1, MS477/3, MS 477/4, MS3881

Trial of Abraham Thornton
Extracts from the 1817 trial of Abraham Thornton at Warwick have been taken from Cooper's *A Report on the Proceedings Against Abraham Thornton* (see Primary Sources), unless otherwise indicated. Descriptions of later proceedings have been taken from multiple newspaper reports, most notably from the *Observer*.

SOURCES

Old Bailey Proceedings Online
Quotations from the trial of David Scott for the rape of Mary Homewood, of John Briant for the rape of Jane Bell and Samuel Mills for the rape of Hannah Whitehorn are from Old Bailey Proceedings Online (www.oldbaileyonline.org). Details of the trial of James Cluff are from www.londonlives.org. For the trial of John Motherhill, see Primary Sources.

Voluntary Examination of Abraham Thornton
This is a transcript of the version included in Edward Sadler's brief for the defence barristers, taken from MS3078/1/8 Folio 33–4.

Omar Hall's Statement
This is the draft of Omar Hall's statement transcribed from MS3069/13/3/72.

Notes & Queries
Mary Ashford's murder remained a subject of speculation and reminiscence for decades after her death and the legal processes that followed. It cropped up frequently amongst the volumes of *Notes & Queries*, a sort of nineteenth-century Wikipedia, specifically Series 2, Vol. 2 (1856), pp. 241-2, 433 and Vol. 11 (1861), pp. 88, 259, 317, 431, and Series 6, Vol. 11 (1885), pp. 144-5, 252, 374, 462-3.

Primary Sources
AMPHLETT, J. (1860). *The Recollections of James Amphlett, Who Has Been Styled the Father of the Press*. London: Whittaker & Co.

ANON. (1796). The Trial of John Motherhill, for the Rape on the Body of Catherine Wade. London: E. Macklew.

ANON. (1817). *Thornton's Trial!! The Trial of Abraham Thornton, at the Warwick Summer Assize, on Friday, the 8th day of August, 1817, for the Murder of Mary Ashford, in the Lordship of Sutton Coldfield... Warwick* (no publisher).

ANON. (1817). *Horrible Rape and Murder!! The Affecting Case of Mary Ashford, A Beautiful Young Virgin Who Was Diabolically Ravished, Murdered, and Thrown in a Pit*. London: John Fairburn.

ANON. (1818). *Appeal of Murder and Trial by Battle*. Quarterly Review. 18 (35), pp. 177-198.

ANON. (John Hiscox) (1818). *An Investigation of the Case of Abraham Thornton, Who Was Tried at Warwick, August 8, 1817, for the Wilful Murder, and Afterwards, Arraigned for the Rape, of Mary Ashford*. London: James Harper.

ANON. (1818?). *On Appeals of Death; Together with a Concise Statement of their Nature*. Birmingham: Richard Jabet.

ANON. (1818). *A Reply to the Remarks of the Rev. Luke Booker, L.L.D. in a Pamphlet Entitled 'A Moral Review' of the Conduct and Case of Mary Ashford, &c. by A Friend to Justice*. Birmingham: W. Suffield.

ANON. (1818). *Thornton's Second Trial*. London: John Fairburn.

ANON. (A Friend to Justice) (1818). *Wager of Battle: Thornton and Mary Ashford; or An Antidote to Prejudice*. London (no publisher).

ANON. (1819?). *Full Report of the Trial of Abraham Thornton for the Wilful Murder of Mary Ashford, at Penn's Mills, near Sutton Coldfield, in the County of Warwick*. Birmingham: Publishing Office.

BARNEWELL, R. V., ALDERSON, E. H. (1818). *Reports of Cases Argued and Determined in the Court of King's Bench*. London: J. Butterworth and Son.

BARR, J. T. (1852). *The Merchant's Daughter and other Narratives*. New York: Lane & Scott.

BECK, T. R., BECK, J. (1836). *Elements of Medical Jurisprudence*. London: Longman.

BEDFORD, W. K. R. (1889). *Three Hundred Years of a Family Living*. Birmingham: Cornish Brothers.

BOOKER, L. (1818). *A Moral Review of the Conduct and Case of Mary Ashford, in refutation of the arguments adduced in defence of her supposed violator and murderer*. Dudley and London: J. Rann; Longman, Hurst & Co.

BORROW, G. (1825). *Celebrated Trials and Remarkable Cases of Criminal Jurisprudence from the Earliest Records to the Year 1825*. London: Knight and Lacey.

COOPER, J. (1818). *A Report of the Proceedings Against Abraham Thornton at Warwick Summer Assizes, 1817, for the Murder of Mary Ashford; and, subsequently, In the Court of King's Bench, in an Appeal of the Said Murder*. Warwick: Heathcote and Foden.

COOPER, J. (1818). *A Report on the Proceedings Against Abraham Thornton, at Warwick Summer Assizes, 1817, for the Murder of Mary Ashford, and subsequently, in the Court of King's Bench in an Appeal of the Said Murder. Warwick: John Cooper.*

CUMMIN, W. (1836). Lectures on Forensic Medicine. *London Medical Gazette* (19), pp. 385-392.

DEFAUCONPRET, A.-J.-B. (1819). *Une Année à Londres*. Paris: Librairie de Gide Fils.

DENT, R. K. D. (1894). *The Making of Birmingham, Being a History of the Rise and Growth of the Metropolis*. Birmingham: J. L. Allday.

SOURCES

DENT, R. K. D. (1880). *Old and New Birmingham: A History of the Town and Its People*. Birmingham: Houghton and Hammond.

HILL, R. & HILL, G. B. (1880). *The Life of Sir Rowland Hill and the History of Penny Postage*. London: Thomas de la Rue & Co.

HINDLEY, C. (1878). *The Life and Times of James Catnach (late of Seven Dials), Ballad Monger*. London: Reeves and Turner.

HUTTON, W., GUEST, J. (1836). *The History of Birmingham*. London: George Berger.

KENDALL, E. A. (1818). *An Argument for Construing Largely the Right of an Appellee of Murder to Insist on Trial by Battle and Also for Abolishing Appeals*. London: Baldwin, Cradock and Joy; Clarke and Sons.

FIELD, W. (1815). *An Historical and Descriptive Account of the Town & Castle of Warwick*. Warwick: H. Sharpe.

LEWIS, S. (1831). *A Topographical Dictionary of England*. London: S. Lewis and Co.

LUDLAM, G. [G. L.] (1817). *The Mysterious Murder: Or, What's the Clock? A Melo-drama in Three Acts … Founded on a Tale Too True*. Birmingham: Taylor.

MALE, G. E. (1816). *An Epitome of Juridical or Forensic Medicine; for the use of medical men, coroners, and barristers*. London: T. & G. Underwood.

MILLER, H. (1851). *First Impressions of England and Its People*. Boston: Gould & Lincoln.

NEILD, J. (1812). *State of the Prisons in England, Scotland and Wales*. London: John Nichols & Son.

PARIS, J. A., FONBLANQUE, J.S.M. (1823). *Medical Jurisprudence*. Edinburgh: Royal College of Physicians of Edinburgh.

PRYME, G. (1870). *Autobiographic Recollections*. Cambridge: Deighton, Bell and Co.

PYE, C. (1820). *A Description of Modern Birmingham. Whereunto Are Annexed Observations Made during an Excursion round the Town in the Summer of 1818, including Warwick and Leamington*. Birmingham, J. Lowe.

REIDER, W. (1841). *The New Tablet of Memory, or Recorder of Remarkable Events*. London: John Clements.

RICHARD, H. (1881). *The Gradual Triumph of Law over Brute Force: A Historic Retrospect*. London: Peace Society (Hodder and Stoughton).

RUTH, R. (1833). *Memoranda of a Residence at the Court of London*. Philadelphia: Key and Biddle.

SMITH, F. (1820). *Warwickshire Delineated; being a concise historial and topographical description of that interesting county*. Southam: Francis Smith.

TIMBS, J. (1868). *London and Westminster: City and Suburb*. London: Richard Bentley.

VAUX, J. H. (1819). *Memoirs of James Hardy Vaux*. London: W. Clowes.

WELLBELOVED, H. (1826). *London Lions for Country Cousins and Friends About Town*. London: William Charlton Wright.

WEST, W. (1830). *History, Topography and Directory of Warwickshire*. Birmingham: Wrighton.

WILLS, W. (1838). *An Essay on the Rationale of Circumstantial Evidence*. London: Longman, Orme, Brown, Green, and Longmans.

WOODALL, W. O. (1873). *A Collection of Reports of Celebrated Trials, Civil and Criminal*. London: Shaw and Sons.

WOOLRYCH, H. W. (1869). *Lives of Eminent Serjeants-at-Law of the English Bar*. London: William H. Allen & Co.

WRIGHTSON, R. (1818). *New Triennial Directory of Birmingham*. Birmingham: R. Wrightson.

YATES, G. (1830). *An Historical and Descriptive Sketch of Birmingham with Some Account of Its Environs*. Birmingham: Beilby, Knott and Beilby.

Select Bibliography

ALLEN, K., & GOLDBERG, A. (2009). Sexual Activity during Menstruation: A Qualitative Study. *The Journal of Sex Research*, 46 (6), pp. 535–545.

AL-KHALIDI, A. (2001). Emergent Technologies in Menstrual Paraphernalia in Mid-Nineteenth-Century Britain. *Journal of Design History*, 14 (4), pp. 257–273.

BAXTER, M. and **DRAKE, P.** (1995). *Images of England: Erdington*. Stroud, Gloucestershire: Tempus Publishing.

BAYARD, R., PAYNE-JAMES, J., eds. (2015). *Encyclopedia of Forensic and Legal Medicine*. Amsterdam: Academic Press.

BEATTIE, J.M. (1986). *Crime and the Courts in England 1600-1800*. Princeton University Press.

BEATTIE, J. M. (1991). Scales of Justice: Defense Counsel and the English Criminal Trial in the Eighteenth and Nineteenth Centuries. *Law and History Review*, 9 (2), pp. 221–267.

BEATTIE, J. M. (2007). Garrow and the Detectives: lawyers and policemen at the Old Bailey in the late eighteenth century. *Crime, Histoire & Sociétés / Crime, History & Societies*, 11 (2), pp. 5–23.

BRADWAY, W. C. (1990). Stages of a sexual assault. *Law and Order*, 38 (9), pp. 119–123.

SOURCES

BRAKE, L., DEMOOR, M. (2009). *Dictionary of Nineteenth-century Journalism in Great Britain and Ireland.* London: Academia Press and British Library.

BURWICK, F. (2011). *Playing to the Crowd: London Popular Theatre (1780-1830).* New York: Palgrave Macmillan.

BUYDENS, N. (2007). *Rape and 'Consent to Force': Legal Doctrine and Social Context in Victorian Britain.* Ph.D. University of Saskatchewan.

CHASSAIGNE, P. (1999). Popular Representations of Crime: The crime broadside — a subculture of violence in Victorian Britain? *Crime, Histoire & Sociétés / Crime, History & Societies,* 3 (2), pp. 23–55.

COOK, E. (2011). *The Damnation of John Donellan: The Mysterious Case of Death & Scandal in Georgian England.* London: Profile Books.

CLARK, A. (1987). *Women's Silence, Men's Violence: Sexual Assault in England 1770-1845.* London: Pandora Press.

DAWSON, D. (2008). *Lovesickness and Gender in Early Modern English Literature.* Oxford: OUP.

D'CRUZE, S. (1992) Approaching the history of rape and sexual violence: notes towards research. *Women's History Review,* 1 (3), pp. 377–397.

DYER, G. R. (1997). 'Ivanhoe', Chivalry, and the Murder of Mary Ashford. *Criticism,* 39 (3), pp. 383–408.

EMSLEY, C. (1996). *Crime and Society in England 1750-1900.* Harlow: Longman.

ERNST, D. R. (1984). The Moribund Appeal of Death: Compensating Survivors and Controlling Jurors in Early Modern England. *The American Journal of Legal History.* 28 (2), pp. 164–188.

FLANDERS, J. (2011). *The Invention of Murder: How the Victorians Revelled in Death and Detection and Created Modern Crime.* London: Harper Press.

FORBES, T. R. (1978). Crowner's Quest. *Transactions of the American Philosophical Society,* 68 (1), pp. 1–52.

FORD, J.M.T. (1987). A Medical Student at St Thomas's Hospital, 1801–1802: The Weekes Family Letters. *Medical History,* (7), pp. 1–30.

GARFIELD, S. (2013). *On the Map: Why the World Looks the Way It Does.* London: Profile Books.

GATTRELL, V.A.C. (1994). *The Hanging Tree: Execution and the English People 1770-1863.* Oxford: OUP.

GIBBONS, P., DE VOLDER, V., CASEY, P. (2003). Patterns of Denial in Sex Offenders. *The Journal of the American Academy of Psychiatry and Law,* 31 (3), pp. 336–334.

GILLIS, J. R. (1979). Servants, Sexual Relations, and the Risks of Illegitimacy in London, 1801–1900. *Feminist Studies,* 5 (1), pp. 142–173.

GRIFFIN, E. (2013). *Liberty's Dawn: A People's History of the Industrial Revolution*. New Haven and London: Yale University Press.

HARVEY, A. D. (1994). *Sex in Georgian England*. London: Phoenix Press.

HAY, D., et al (1975). *Albion's Fatal Tree*. London: Peregrine.

HAYES, P. (2002). *One Morning in May: The Mary Ashford Mystery*. Studley, Warwickshire: Brewin Books.

HIBBERT, C. (1963). *The Roots of Evil: A Social History of Crime and Punishment*. London: Weidenfeld & Nicolson.

HOLLMAN, A. (2001). Postmortems on the Kitchen Table. *BMJ*, 323 (7327), pp. 1472–1473.

HOLMES, R.M. & HOLMES, S.T. (2009). *Sex Crimes: Patterns and Behavior*. Thousand Oaks, California: Sage Publications.

HOLMES, R.M. & HOLMES, S.T. (2009). *Profiling Violent Crimes: An Investigative Tool*. Thousand Oaks, California: Sage Publications.

HOLMSTROM, L.L., BURGESS, A.W. (1980). Sexual behavior of assailants during reported rapes. *Archives of Sexual Behaviour*, 9 (5), pp. 427–???.

HORSFALL, J. (1971). *The Iron Masters of Penns*. Kineton: The Roundwood Press.

JONES, D. V. (1985). *The Story of Erdington: from Sleepy Hamlet to Thriving Suburb*. Sutton Coldfield: Westwood Press.

KING, P. (2006). *Crime and Law in England, 1750-1840: Remaking Justice from the Margins*. Cambridge: CUP.

KING, P. (2000). *Crime, Justice and Discretion in England, 1740-1820*. Oxford: OUP.

KIRK, M. S. (1934). 'Jeopardy' During the Period of the Year Books. *University of Pennsylvania Law Review and American Law Register*. 82 (6). pp. 602–617.

LANGBEIN, J. H. (1993). The Historical Origins of the Privilege Against Self-Incrimination at Common Law. *Michigan Law Review*, 92, pp. 1047–1085.

LOGAN, G. (1928). *Guilty or Not Guilty: Stories of Celebrated Crimes*. London: Stanley Paul Co.

MANCHESTER, C. (1978). Wives as Crown Witnesses. *The Cambridge Law Journal*, 37 (2), pp. 249–251.

MCCABE, M.P., WAUCHOPE, M. (2005). Behavioural characteristics of rapists, *Journal of Sexual Aggression*, 11 (3), pp. 235–247.

MCLYNN, F. (1991). *Crime and Punishment in Eighteenth-Century England*. Oxford: OUP.

MAY, A. S. (2003). *The Bar & the Old Bailey 1750–1850*. Chapel Hill and London: University of North Carolina Press.

SOURCES

MEGARRY, R. E. (2005). *A New Miscellany-at-Law*. Oxford and Portland, Oregon: Hart Publishing.

MILKA, A., LEMMINGS, D. (2017) Narratives of Feeling and Majesty: Mediated Emotions in the Eighteenth-Century Criminal Courtroom, *The Journal of Legal History*, 38 (2), pp. 155–178.

NUTT, T. (2010). Illegitimacy, Paternal Financial Responsibility, and the 1834 Poor Law Commission Report: The Myth of the Old Poor Law and the Making of the New. *The Economic History Review*, 63 (2), pp. 335–361.

PISANI, M. V. (2014). *Music for the Melodramatic Theatre in Nineteenth-Century London and New York*. Iowa City: University of Iowa Press.

PORTER, R. (1982). *English Society in the Eighteenth Century*. London: Penguin.

PORTER, R. (1986). Rape – Does it Have a Historical Meaning? In: Tomaselli, S., Porter, R., *Rape: An Historical and Social Enquiry*. Oxford: Basil Blackwell.

ROSE, R. (1960). The Priestley Riots of 1791. *Past & Present*, 18, pp. 68–88.

RIDDELL, W. R. (1926). Appeal of Death and Its Abolition. *Michigan Law Review*. 24 (8), pp. 786–808.

READ, S. (2015). *Maids, Wives, Widows: Exploring Early Modern Women's Lives*. Barnsley: Pen & Sword.

ROE, N. (2005). *Fiery Heart: The First Life of Leigh Hunt*. London: Pimlico.

ROGERS, N. (1989). Carnal Knowledge: Illegitimacy in Eighteenth-Century Westminster. *Journal of Social History*, 23 (2), pp. 355–375.

RUDÉ, G. (1985). *Criminal and Victim: Crime and Society in Early Nineteenth-Century England*. Oxford: Clarendon Press.

RULE, J. (1992). *Albion's People: English Society 1714-1815*. Harlow: Longman.

RULE, J. (1986). *The Labouring Classes in Early Industrial England 1750-1850*. Harlow: Longman.

SCHOENFIELD, M. (2000). Waging Battle: Ashford v. Thornton, Ivanhoe, and Legal Violence, *Prose Studies*, 23 (2), pp.61–86.

SHOEMAKER, R. B. (2002). The taming of the duel: masculinity, honour and ritual violence in London 1600-1800. *The Historical Journal*, 45 (3), pp. 525–545.

SHOWALTER, E., & SHOWALTER, E. (1970). Victorian Women and Menstruation. *Victorian Studies*, 14(1), pp. 83–89.

SIMPSON, A. (1986). The 'Blackmail Myth' and the Prosecution of Rape and Its Attempt in 18th Century London: The Creation of a Legal Tradition. *The Journal of Criminal Law and Criminology*, 77 (1), pp. 101–150.

STEELE, E. B. (2012). *Material Murders: 'Authenticity' in Early Nineteenth-Century True Crime Murder Melodrama*. Ph.D. University of Maryland.

STUDD, J. (2007). A comparison of 19th century and current attitudes to female sexuality. *Gynecological Endocrinology*, 23 (1), pp. 673–681.

WIENER. M. J. (1999) Judges v. Jurors: Courtroom Tensions in Murder Trials and the Law of Criminal Responsibility in Nineteenth-Century England. *Law and History Review*, 17 (3), pp. 467–506.

WEINER, M. J. (2001). Alice Arden to Bill Sikes: Changing Nightmares of Intimate Violence in England, 1558-1869. *Journal of British Studies*, 40 (2), pp. 184–212.

WEINER, M. J. (2004). *Men of Blood: Violence, Manliness, and Criminal Justice in Victorian England.* Cambridge: CUP.

WILKES, S. (2014). *Jane Austen's England.* Barnsley: Pen & Sword.

WORRALL, D. (2006). *Theatric Revolution: Drama, Censorship and Romantic Period Subcultures 1773–1832.* Oxford: OUP.